DISCOVER THE
ETERNAL YOU!

TRAVEL THE PATH TOWARD GOD CONSCIOUSNESS

DR. ANNA ZIBARRAS, PHD

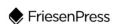 FriesenPress

One Printers Way
Altona, MB R0G 0B0
Canada

www.friesenpress.com

ISBN
978-1-03-915486-5 (Hardcover)
978-1-03-915485-8 (Paperback)
978-1-03-915487-2 (eBook)

1. SELF-HELP, SPIRITUAL

Distributed to the trade by The Ingram Book Company

Disclaimer

Nothing mentioned in this book should be considered as infallible. The ideas and views expressed herein, may be used in one's spiritual life for the purpose of awakening to truths and ideals, in addition to one's spiritual beliefs.

Dedication

This book is dedicated to my beloved husband for his valuable contribution to the writing of this book, to my most precious children, and to my wonderful grandchildren. May the ideas mentioned in these pages help them advance their consciousness and realize spiritual fulfillment and enlightenment in their lives.

TABLE OF CONTENTS

PREFACE

"It is no mark of intelligence to be able to prove
whatever one pleases. But to be able to discern
what is true as true and what is false as false—this
is the mark and character of intelligence."
Emmanuel Swedenborg

THE PURPOSE OF THIS BOOK is to show that by
gaining knowledge in metaphysics and in mysticism, we
can develop our spiritual nature to such an extent that we
can achieve improved health, increased inner happiness, and
greater success in our lives.

My aim is to share the knowledge I gained from my
formal university studies and from my life experiences with
anyone who seeks a more spiritually enlightened life.

During the process of writing this book, I experienced a
personal spiritual awakening. I found profound peace and
joy. I learned that the best way to know God was to know
myself first by observing my inner being in deep silence. I

learned how to analyze and examine the real motives behind my thoughts, words, and actions.

What I would like to do in the next few pages is to clarify the ideas of our outer and of our inner self. It is to guide the reader to the discovery of the Kingdom of Heaven within and to the realization of our inner divine self.

INTRODUCTION

"It is the mark of an educated mind to be able to
entertain a thought without accepting it."

Aristotle

I WAS BORN AND RAISED in a deeply religious
Christian home.

My family has belonged for generations to the Greek
Orthodox Christian faith. Their beliefs, religious rituals, and
their traditions have influenced greatly my mindset.

I learned to pray at quite a young age. I prayed twice a day,
once every morning before breakfast and once every evening
before going to bed. I fasted regularly and kept asking God
daily for health, guidance, prosperity, and protection for me
and for my family.

By the time I became a teenager, I knew in my heart, that
God was present in my life. I believed that He was more
loving and more benevolent than what most people seem to
think or believe.

I had noticed that some people seemed to be luckier in life than others. Everything seemed to be going the right way for them. They had good health, good relationships and abundant prosperity in their lives. For others, though, their lives were a mixture of good and bad days, happy and unhappy times. I kept thinking, "what are the factors that distinguish good lives from difficult ones?"

Based on my personal experiences, I was convinced that our supplications are heard and that there is a definite response from the universe to our prayers and wishes.

I came to believe that nothing happens in this universe by coincidence or by chance. I noticed that there is too much order in the cosmos, for one to believe that things can happen at random and out of control.

As I reached adulthood and after having read many spiritual books and spoken to highly spiritual people, I realized that we are more than physical beings and that we do exist in more than one dimension. We exist simultaneously in the physical dimension—which constitutes the visible realm—as well as in the higher dimension of mind and spirit, which constitute its invisible counterpart.

How do we achieve a balance between those two dimensions without going to extremes in either direction and without neglecting the basic spiritual values in life or our everyday physical necessities?

I was amazed with the idea that there is the possibility of a more perfect knowledge of God in this life, through which the soul is able to contemplate directly the mysteries of the divine presence, which is the Kingdom of Heaven within.

As time went by, my inner self continued to press upon me to study ways of getting closer to the infinite presence of God. I started searching for a spiritual path which would lead me there. I kept looking for practical ways that I could use in my everyday life in order to progress spiritually.

As I progressed on this path through meditation, prayer, and my formal university studies, I came across concepts such as elevated consciousness, elevated awareness, spiritual unity, inner peace, and divine harmony. This made me very excited and more interested. I was extremely curious to discover and experience more of each and every one of these concepts.

What I found fascinating was that most, if not all, of the spiritual paths such as Christianity, Buddhism, and so on, teach high moral discipline as the main path to opening one's consciousness to the divine. Moral discipline is the conscious awareness and determination to avoid acts that cause harm to oneself or others, while trying to achieve virtuous acts that benefit all.

I started reading the teachings of esoteric Christianity as well as the teachings of other esoteric philosophies. The more I researched, the more impressed and interested I became. I felt an inward urge to discover concepts of spiritual truths that would help me reach elevated state of spiritual unity with the Universal Mind.

What was the secret of "the Kingdom" Jesus spoke of? I wondered. What did he mean when he said to his disciples,

"The secret of the Kingdom of God has been given to you. But to those on the outside everything is said in parables" (Mark 4:11).

Also, what was the deeper message of his teaching? "But seek first his kingdom and his righteousness, and all these things will be given to you as well" (Matthew 6:33). How do I reach the Kingdom of Heaven? I wondered.

The idea of being able to reach "holiness" in this lifetime amazed and excited me for a very long time. I was convinced that the purpose of our life on Earth was to achieve holiness and to experience the Kingdom of Heaven or the presence of God within while we are still in the physical body. We read in the Bible, "Make every effort to live in peace with everyone and to be holy; without sovereignty no one will see the Lord" (Hebrews 12:14).

I realized, that through time, the concept of God has changed, in different parts of the world. The old prevalent image of God as an omnipotent, intelligent Creator distant from the world has gradually changed to the image of a universal, all-pervading, unifying energy at the centre of the Cosmos. This perception of the nature of the universe as one unified whole makes us see the divine and the humanity as just different dimensions of one vast sacred mystery, worth searching for and finding.

My genuine need to get to know my true, divine self-better and deeper made me start to observe myself systematically, to watch my thoughts and feelings more intensely and to become more mindful of everything I did. This continuous mindfulness, in conjunction with my increased meditation practices, changed the way I perceived my life. It enabled me to recognize the different physical and metaphysical manifestations that were presenting themselves to me as miracles and as cases of spiritual healing and synchronicity.

I noticed that some mystical divine energy was influencing all the aspects of my life. It was increasing my conscious awareness levels and improving my intuition to a great extent. That made me realize and accept the fact that faith, devotion, meditation, and prayer can expand our awareness. It can lead us to higher states of consciousness. It can open new horizons in us and allow us to transcend our limited, personal ego-dominated consciousness.

Eventually, it became evident to me that the human mind, by the very special grace of God, is able to connect directly into the mysteries of the divine presence. It is able to discover the path to communion with God, to mystical experiences, and to spiritual development, which eventually lead the devotee to absolute happiness and bliss in life.

I have divided this book into six sections or aspects of our being, namely into the physical aspect, the mental aspect, the emotional aspect, the psychic aspect, and the divine aspect. I tried to analyze and to share with you my knowledge about our physical self, about our brain, and about our mind, which is part of the soul. I tried to explain that we all are part of the one universal energy and that our thoughts, feelings and emotions shape up our life and our future. I mentioned that through faith, meditation, prayer and virtuous acts, we can achieve higher spiritual states, have mystical experiences and encounter miracles in our lives.

I emphasized that through the study of metaphysics and mysticism, we can expand our consciousness and reach the desired state of connecting with God, which will lead us to holiness.

If we aspire to go beyond the present state of consciousness, if we want to experience other higher dimensions, we should look beyond matter and beyond the illusionary manifestation of this reality. We should look beyond the veil of form and try to achieve the realization of oneness between us, the universe, and everything else. This will lead us to love and know ourselves better and to regain meaning and wholeness in our lives.

PART ONE

The Physical Aspect

"More smiling, less worrying. More compassion,
less judgment. More blessed, less stressed.
More love, less hate."

Roy T. Bennett

CHAPTER ONE

"Each person has a self-image that, to some degree,
does not match reality. A significant difference
between self-image and reality can be harmful."
Robert H. Bolton and Dorothy Grover Bolton

THE SELF

The self is who a person thinks he is. It gives the individual
his sense of personal identity as a human being, and it forms
the foundation of all his behaviour.

The self asks questions such as Who am I? Why do I
occupy myself with so many different thoughts? Why do
I need to calculate and analyze everything, and why can I
not let chance determine things? Why do I think about my
actions before I perform them? Is it because I want to avoid
pain? Is it because I want to receive acceptance?

After extensive academic as well as inner searching, I
realized that we are the visible parts of an invisible whole.
We exist as physical beings in a physical world while our

mind is in continuous communication with unseen forces and unseen worlds.

We all have two separate selves: our rational, conscious, responsible side; and our instinctual, subconscious, and emotional side. In order to have a harmonious totality and a balanced personality, we need to discover our two separate selves and to balance them. We need to take care of both sides of our personality equally. We need to be reflective of our goals and be organized, responsible, and logical but at the same time, we need not ignore our artistic, creative, and emotional side.

Know Thyself

Have you ever thought about why it is so important to know yourself? Is it to accept yourself? Is it to improve your self-image?

Most of us do not know who we are. The illusion of self has made us forget our real, true selves. When Socrates said the famous "Know thyself" what did he exactly mean? Most humans live their daily lives with little thought about who they are and why they are here. Most of us have never realized our higher, real selves, or our soul, which is beyond matter and form and beyond thinking. We believe that we are these biological bodies that are limited in time and space. Well, this form that we all identify with is part of the ego construct, which always strives for more money, more power, more love, and more of everything until it dies sooner or later.

Most of us think that we are what we have been told to be by our society and by our culture. Consequently, our thoughts and actions are governed by our deeper unconscious biological desires and impulses and by our subconscious thoughts and emotions. We keep fulfilling our basic needs, our social, religious and financial obligations. We keep trying to satisfy our ideas, our beliefs, and our desires, but in spite of all these, we still feel anxiety, self-doubt and fear of change and criticism.

I strongly believe that our aim in life should be to discover who we really are. It is to know our true selves, our purpose in life, and our connection to the Universe. Without this knowledge of ourselves, we are solely governed by past conditionings, by thoughts that are not even our own, and by attitudes and beliefs that we have adopted from our culture, from our family, and our society.

In order to know who, we really are, we need first to make the distinction between our two selves which are:

1. The true or higher self, which is eternal, pure and close to the all-loving presence of God and

2. The false, limited self, which is temporary and associated with our earthly personality. It is the product of our interactions with society. It leads us to live captive to the expectations of others. This often gives us a sense of inadequacy and insecurity.

The need to turn to our true self often emerges in times of great self-doubt and of great difficulties. That is the time that we are more open to listen to the voice inside us.

The Ego Self

We humans in the physical realm experience ourselves, our thoughts, and our feelings as something separate from Nature and from other human beings. This is Nature's best deception and a kind of a delusion caused by our ego.

It is not so much the outer circumstances that limit us as the state of consciousness that dominates our thinking. Our thinking creates our feelings, our emotions, our attitudes, and our actions. Our thinking controls the brain waves that we transmit and the frequencies of our vibrations. It controls our lives, our financial livelihood, and our destiny.

Our physical lives are truly wasted if they are driven just by our ego. By only chasing pleasure and avoiding pain, we become slaves to the forces of our ego personality, and our real life and values remain unknown to us. When we become aware of this situation and we realize that we are identifying solely with our illusionary self, we will be awakened and be able to act freely without been driven by unconscious motives.

Without an awakened consciousness, any knowledge or understanding attained by the ego self would be dangerous and disconnected from higher wisdom.

Life After Death

The concept of life after death is a concept created by the collective human mind to help people deal with the fear of death. It has been used by various religions in order to control the behaviour of individuals through reward and punishment in the afterlife. When we experience the truth of our immortal and eternal higher self, there will be no longer any fear of death.

Before we can talk about life after death though, let us first understand what is the reality of life, and let us realize that life and death are inseparable. They are parts of an endless continuum with no beginning and no end. This means that if we eliminate the idea of death, we will need to forget the idea of life too.

What Is Your Physical Life?

Is your physical life your name? Is it your personality? Is it your profession? Is it your relationships? Is it your health, or is it your social and cultural values? Sure, all of the above are part of your conceptual life, but are they life itself?

As long as we are alive, the coexistence of our mind with our body gives us the identity that we have. This same identity carries on throughout our lives, although both our bodies and our personalities undergo huge changes. We do not look like what we looked twenty, thirty, or forty years ago, neither we feel nor we behave the same way.

We humans have created our own concepts of our bodies, of success and failure, of love and hate, of poverty and wealth, and so on. These concepts and the sense of solidity that we have about our bodies are not real. They do not really exist outside the world of our thoughts. They are the product of our own mind and convictions only. They are part of an idea or a self-image that is only real to us and to nobody else. They are created by us and by our physical and social environment.

They are subject to change relative to changes around us. They belong to the illusionary aspect of the human mind, which creates a conceptual life. That is not *real* life.

An Allegorical Story by Socrates, Written by Plato
Socrates once told his student Plato a story about several prisoners who have lived their entire lives chained in a dark cave.

> Behind the men there was a fire, and between the fire and the prisoners there were people, animals, and other objects. All those cast fearful shadows on the opposite wall of the cave. The prisoners believing that the shadows were real, lived in terror and fear. The shadows on the wall were their only reality, as they knew nothing else.
>
> One prisoner happened to break free from the cave. He fought his way through the darkness and emerged into the sunlight of the real world. He saw the fire and realized that the shadows were fake and that there was a whole new world outside and a new reality that he was previously unaware of.
>
> What would happen if he were to try to return to the cave and tell the prisoners of his discovery? What would happen, if he had explained to them that their fear and pain was the result of their illusions? Would they have believed that an

DR. ANNA ZIBARRAS, PH.D

entirely new world existed on the outside? Would they have welcomed his message? They probably wouldn't have. Why should they give up their assumptions about what is real? No, they would have called him a fool and remained in despair. (Plato 2017, 253-261)

The story of the cave is an allegorical presentation of how most people live in the world. They are not aware of the difference of what is real, what is truth, and what is just an interpretation of reality and of the truth produced in their minds. Lack of awareness makes us fearful and causes us to believe that truth is not worth seeking. We fear that it may even be harmful to our habitual ways of thinking and acting.

Death of the physical body
A hundred times every day, I remind myself that each of us is here for a brief sojourn. We do not know what our purpose in life is, but we sometimes sense that we exist for other people, for their smiles and well-being.

It is a very encouraging thought to consider that if all matter is merely energy condensed into a slower vibration, then we are all part of the one and only source of energy in the universe. That energy merely manifests differently in each one of us. Hence, there is no such thing as death because energy never dissipates.

Nature has a soothing effect on the soul, because through it, we feel connected to the source of our creation and to every other creature. Nature is not something that is separate from us. We are all part of it.

At the moment of death, when the physical body separates from the soul and the thought-producing brain ceases to exist, all our bodily convictions, sense-related experiences, and realities cease to exist. Our bodies return to Earth, where they get recycled by insects and bacteria and become part of something else on the planet.

The only experience we have at the time of our death is the experience of our consciousness—of our spiritual awareness and of the mental tendencies and experiences that we have created during our lives.

Real Life

Real life is not a concept created by the human mind. It is the energy that flows through every life form. It is what makes every living being alive. It is what we were born with, and what we lose at the end of our material life. It is what makes the difference between a living and a dead form.

In a mystical sense, there is but one life in the Universe, and there is but one universal soul, whose body is light energy. This means that all creatures have originated from that one energy in a higher spiritual realm before manifesting in the physical form.

Life is neither long nor short, neither good nor bad. Life never ends, just as energy never ends. It gets transformed, but it does not disappear. The form dies but life does not. The opposite of life is not death; birth is the opposite of death. Life has no opposite. Life just is.

We can sense our life flowing through us if we sit still, switch off our busy thinking mind, and turn our attention to our chest and to our each and every breath. If we try to sense the energy flowing through our body, we will feel an enormous sense of peace, love and harmony inside us and all around us.

During our sleep, we experience sights, though not through our physical eyes, as our eyes are shut. Our mind is what observes and witnesses these images, emotions and experiences. It is therefore logical to conclude that the mind, which survives the physical death of the body, is not dependent on our brain and on our five senses.

After death, our mind which is part of the soul or our consciousness, continues to feel emotions in the same way that we experience them in our sleep and dream state. The kind of emotions that our consciousness experiences after it leaves the physical body makes the difference between the states of consciousness that we call paradise or hell. If the emotions are happy and positive, it is heaven or paradise, or if they are painful and guilt ridden, it is hell. On the other hand, if the soul is free of any emotional burden, it will be neither paradise nor hell but the state of eternity and bliss.

Living Consciously

The conscious mind makes us see reality through the personal lens of our perception. If our perception is distorted due to false statements, untrue facts and malicious presentations, then our reality through the lens of our perception tricks us, and it generates stressful emotions. This distortion of awareness is based on our cultural values, on our belief systems, on our preconceived ideas based on our upbringing, and on the experiences, we have of the outer world.

For example, some amazing, successful people consider themselves unworthy and failures because of unrealistic expectations set on them by society, and they are promoted on social media. They tend to exaggerate their weaknesses and minimize their strengths. Many young people kill themselves because of bullying, which causes chronic self-criticism, low self-esteem, and changes in the way they see themselves.

The only way to control our conscious mind from the uncontrollable flow of thoughts and ideas is to start observing the games it plays on us. In other words, we need to observe the flow of the different, continuous thoughts that are passing through our minds and their physiological and psychological effects on us. Understanding, controlling and directing our minds and thoughts in an orderly way is the only way to a peaceful life and a solution to unhappy moments and depressed moods.

Try and block your undesirable, hurtful, agitating and negative thoughts and replace them with positive, promising and joyful ones. By doing that, you will eliminate the negative effects on your bodies, your lives and your environments and will replace them with positive effects.

Mindful Living

Mindful living, conscious living, or inner attention is our ability to be fully conscious of every moment that goes by. It is our ability to be fully aware of every activity, thought, or emotion that is experienced in our mind at that moment while remaining unaffected by it.

Conscious living is the process of keeping one's attention focused on the present reality and, hence, of being awakened to life. It is an exercise in maintaining calmness and developing a deeper consciousness and a higher sensitive awareness. It is a way of getting out of our subjective world and of starting to experience a more objective reality.

One way of achieving conscious and joyful living is by stopping the turmoil of anxiety-provoking thoughts in our minds and by fixing our attention and awareness onto our present state of being or onto the present activity.

We need to learn to experience each activity in our day with enthusiasm and freshness as if it were happening for the first time, without comparing the present experience to the past experiences. Comparing means drawing from our memories and becoming victims of our subjective mind, hence experiencing boredom, dullness, fear, and anxiety.

Artist, educator, nun, and advocate for social justice, Corita Kent (1918-1986), published a notebook to be used by both men, women, and children, as a journal, diary, or composition book for school and work, called Life *is a succession of moments. To live, each one is to succeed* (Kent 2020). The present is the moment that creates our future. Our future and our past depend on our ability to handle the present. If we manage to handle the present moment successfully and effectively by practising a mystical oneness with God, then we will be creating a happy future and a happy life for ourselves.

Living consciously is the opposite to responding automatically to external stimuli or to our internal emotions. It is to be aware of the present moment. Being aware and conscious of the present moment, combined with inner attention to a higher reality, are the only means to spiritual awakening and to the inflow of a higher energy into our being.

Be consciously aware of your feelings and emotions instead of suppressing them before blocking the undesirable, negative thoughts, and replacing them with positive, joyful thoughts. Suppressed feelings and emotions create neurotic situations, but conscious blocking of negative thoughts relieves stress and anxiety.

Develop the ability to observe yourself-as well as your thoughts and emotions as they occur-by identifying yourself with your true higher self. If you notice that certain people drain your positive energy, avoid their company, as it will be destructive to your energy field. The more mindfully and consciously we live in the present time, the more we will understand the spiritual planes of existence, which dominate our whole being.

If we practice "being" rather than "doing" and enjoy every moment of it, we will not have to do anything or go anywhere. It will never be necessary to hurry or rush our precious life away.

Forget the past, forget the people who belonged to your past, they are part of history. Ignore the future; it is the unknown, full of "ifs" and "whens." Concentrate on the *present*. It is the only thing that you can control and change. Eckhart Tolle, a German-born spiritual teacher and self-help author, wrote, "Our endless thoughts often focus on the past or the future. However, we have no control over either — the past is over and the future isn't here yet — so we are in an endless cycle of wasting our mental and emotional energy on things we can't control. The only moment we can impact is the present" (Tolle Eckhart, 2022 on line).

Our breath

Our breath, our emotions, our mind, and our body are interconnected. Breath is the connecting link between matter, energy, consciousness, and mind. It leads us into a higher consciousness. When the body is calm, the breath is calm; when the body is agitated or tired, our exhalation becomes forceful and heavy. When we are surprised or shocked, we draw quick breaths. When we attempt intense concentration, we hold our breath. When we are excited, our inhalation is enthusiastic.

When we focus on our breathing, we use the breath as an object of concentration and of meditation. Concentrating on our breathing reminds us to come back to the present moment so that we create a harmonious awareness between body and mind. It is an excellent way to reduce restlessness and anxiety and improve our physical and mental states of health.

If we practice mindfulness of breathing throughout our daily routine and especially when we experience mental disturbances and anxiety, we will experience internal peace irrespective of what the problem may be.

CHAPTER TWO

"...And when the brain dies, the
person goes out of existence."
Pinker

THE BRAIN

What is the brain and how does it affect the different organs in our body and our life in general?

The brain is an extremely complex structure with different parts which work together in order to process information received from the world as well as from the rest of the body.

The brain controls all the body functions of a human being. It receives and radiates physical, spiritual and psychic energy.

The brain and the mind, or consciousness, are two separate entities. Our brain processes the information that it receives:

- from the outer objective world, through our five senses, and also
- from our inner subjective, intuitive world.

Our intellect is a function of our brain. It helps us to make decisions in order to survive successfully within the constantly changing outer circumstances of our life.

Our brain has been conditioned by us to see the outer reality in a very limited way. When we focus our attention on this three-dimensional reality, our brain narrows its focus onto everything material. This is called a conversion focus.

When we are worried and anxious, the hormones of stress which are released in our bodies amplify that process of conversion focus onto the stress provoking thoughts causing more stress and more anxiety in us.

Brain Waves

I find the knowledge of the various brain waves to be terribly interesting! It helps me understand how my brain works, and it enables me to regulate my brain waves in order to focus better, meditate easier, fall asleep faster, and experience expanded states of consciousness.

When neurons fire in our brain, they create electromagnetic frequencies, which we can capture by using electro-encephalogram (EEG) readings. If we can understand the different brain waves, we can control them more easily.

Our different brain waves are classified as the delta, theta, alpha, beta and gamma. We can think of the beta and alpha waves as the seat of our conscious mind and the gamma, the theta, and delta waves representing our subconscious and our superconscious mind, which transcends ordinary human consciousness.

Delta brain waves range from 0.5 Hz to 4 Hz. Those are the slowest brain waves that we can achieve when there is very little activity in the conscious mind. They take place during our deepest, dreamless stages of sleep, allowing the brain to rest and restore itself.

Theta brain waves range from 4 Hz to 8 Hz. It is the stage we are in, when we are daydreaming or falling asleep, or semi asleep. It is the hypnotic state when our susceptibility increases and our ability to analyze decreases. At this stage, we are open to any suggestion because the seat of our conscious mind, our identity and our personality are suppressed.

Alpha brain waves range between 8 Hz to 12 Hz. They are the waves that are produced when we are idle and physically and mentally relaxed, when we meditate, practice yoga, or read. Often our brain switches from beta waves to alpha waves when we disconnect from our outer environment for a minute and we lose focus on what we are busy doing. That is the time when our inner world becomes more real than the outer world, when our focus shifts away from the analytical stage to the automatic trans stage, when the imagination takes over, when our senses shut off temporarily, and our subconscious takes over.

Beta brain waves range between 12 Hz to 32 Hz. They are the waves that operate at high frequencies when we are awake and aware. It is the stage of being conscious of our bodies in space and time, when we see, hear, taste, smell, feel, and experience. The beta brain waves help us think logically when we work and when we socialize with other people.

We emit beta brain waves when we get aroused or when we experience fear, stress, or anxiety. When there is an overflow of the stress hormone in our body, the brain moves to the frequency of a high beta state, and we behave erratically or speak incoherently.

Gamma brain waves range from 32 Hz to 100 Hz. They have the highest and most rare frequency of all the other brain waves. The frequency of gamma waves is faster and more condensed than beta waves. They occur when we are at peak perception and expanded levels of consciousness and when a non-stress related arousal takes place in the brain. When the arousal is due to a higher energy, the brain moves to a superconscious and to a super-aware state producing emotions like ecstasy, bliss and euphoria. In that state our inner world becomes more important than our outer world.

PART TWO

The Mental Aspect

"Believe in your infinite potential. Your only
limitations are those you set upon yourself."
Roy T. Bennett

CHAPTER THREE

"A mind that is full of conclusions is a dead
mind, it is not a living mind. A living mind is
a free mind, learning, never concluding."

Krishnamurti

THE MIND

If we could only understand the power of our conscious,
subconscious, and superconscious mind, we would spend
much more time finding out how our mind works and how
we can have more control over our lives.

Based on the theory of "Dualism" by the famous French
philosopher Descartes of the seventeenth century, matter
and mind do coexist and interact, although they are of different nature. We have talents and abilities within us that
we are not aware of. Inside our mind lies the cause of almost
everything that enters our lives. Our mind has the ability to
act like a powerful magnet, attracting and repelling situations, things, and people to us and away from us. So, negative

thinking seems to attract negative experiences, and positive thinking seems to produce desirable experiences.

According to mystics, the human mind and the human brain are two separate entities. The human mind is part of the intelligent Universal Mind that exists in the entire Universe and which is all-powerful, all-creative, all-knowing, and always present. Non-mystics, though, believe that the mind is a function of the brain.

The meaning of "mind" in our everyday life refers to two things. First, it refers to our intellect, which is an instrument of survival in the physical world. Our intellect largely functions out of consciously perceived data and out of the different existing levels of memory. It processes the sensory perceptions that our brain receives through our five senses. Consequently, if there is no perceived data, and when our memory fails, our intellect cannot function.

The second reference that defines our mind is our identity, which is protected by our intellect. If our identity gets threatened by an internal or external cause, our intellect gets activated in order to protect it, therefore our intellect serves our identity.

Our Universe is a huge field of energy. We are all individual systems of energy fields within it, which interact with each other and with the environment at large. The auras around our bodies and the meridians of our bodies are examples of our energy fields. The rate at which the human energy fields relate to the other energy fields around us determines our health, our well-being, and our life experiences.

Every act and every thought, when done out of love and out of spiritual awareness and compassion activates some great forces that make a huge positive difference in our lives, in the lives of others, and in the world at large. In the same way, any negative thoughts or actions produce negative consequences and experiences for all of us.

The Universal Mind, or God, is a unified energy field that connects all minds with each other. Every single one of us is part of that energy field, so we are all connected and part of the same one Mind. All metaphysical teachings teach that there is one mind in the universe and that all minds are individual expressions of that one mind and inseparable parts of it. Based on this theory, we all have access to each other's minds and to the mind of God.

Many people have not realized that the ability to connect with this universal mind is within them. It lies beyond the turbulence that exists in their conscious mind, which is caused by their attention and focus to their daily external activities only. They have not realized what it is, how it works, or how it produces miracles in the lives of those who are connected to it.

By constantly striving to contact the Universal Mind of God, we cause the release of such a powerful energy in our minds that our prayer becomes the most powerful tool a human being can possess.

By directing our thought activity solely towards God and away from any external stimulation around us, we can feel the positive transformation in our beings.

The Levels of The Human Mind

There are three independent levels in our minds. They all have their own importance, and they are interrelated.

The conscious mind, which can hold one thought at a time as it has no memory. It is equivalent to the RAM in our computer system. We are in the conscious level of our mind when we are busy with our daily activities and when we are aware of ourselves and of our surroundings. Our conscious mind is also at work when we receive, analyze, and process the information from our environment through our five senses.

The subconscious level of our mind, which is equivalent to the hard disk in our computers. Our subconscious mind is where everything is stored since our birth. Our experiences, our values, our talents, our feelings, our emotions, and everything else are stored in there. Depending on its contents, our subconscious mind controls the way we perceive our outer world through our conscious mind.

When our conscious mind merges with our subconscious mind, we begin to connect with our autonomous nervous system and we say that we move beyond the self. When we get beyond the self and beyond everything that is known in the three-dimensional reality, our brain, heart, and body start working in a coherent, integrated, and orderly way, resulting in better health, peace and joy.

We can only control and deal with whatever is in our conscious mind. Whatever emotion, desire, fear or guilt is not brought up from the subconscious level of our mind to our conscious level, it cannot be dealt by us.

The following true story is an example of the merging of the conscious and the subconscious minds. My friend was suffering from depression and anxiety for ten long years following the death of her son. She had not been sleeping well, and she was on antidepressants. In my effort to help her, I gave her weekly sessions of metaphysical counselling for several months. I explained to her how to open herself to the divine or universal energy and how to channel healing to her mind, body, and spirit. I showed her how to get beyond the three-dimensional reality and how to connect her conscious mind to the subconscious and superconscious parts of it in order to achieve self-healing peace and joy. Gradually, her panic attacks became fewer and fewer, and they eventually stopped. She could sleep better, enjoy life more, and stopped the antidepressant medication.

There are many activities in our body that we are not aware of. Our internal organs perform many extremely complex functions. Nearly 1,000,000 cells are dying every second in our body. Before dying, they copy the genetic code into the new cells.

Most people are not aware of the contents or the power of their subconscious mind. They do not realize that their thinking is what directs and shapes their lives.

Our subconscious mind

- records every activity that we are engaged in before our conscious mind is aware of it,

- records what we think and feel about anything and everything,
- records all our past memories, past experiences, likes, dislikes, fears, phobias, and beliefs. It contains our preconceived ideas and it is responsible for each person's own interpretations of events and automatic reactions to them,
- records information, which is stored there through our emotions, our imagination, or our dreams.

The **superconscious mind** is the highest level of consciousness. It deals with a level of awareness which is beyond material reality. It is the level of intuition, of creativity, of healing, and of spiritual experiences. It is the level at which we attract thoughts and information from the universe.

- When we are in the superconscious level,
- we see all things, living and non-living as one,
- we experience divine love and bliss,
- we see the underlying unity in everything, and
- we realize that everything is made up of the same energy at the most basic level and that everything is interconnected deeply.

Mind Awareness

Awareness is a perception of the mind, and it cannot exist without the mind. Whatever exists only as awareness to our mind is subjective, deceptive, and transitory, and it does not have a real existence. In other words, it is what we call an illusion. The twentieth century French philosopher and

Nobel prize winner for literature, Jan-Paul Sartre, said that the moment we realize that we are not immortal, we see the meaning of life as an illusion.

As humans, we live in a world built on illusions, whether we are awake or asleep. When we are awake, our awareness is based on the illusion of our five senses in the conscious part of our mind. When we are asleep, dreams are based on the contents and illusions of our subconscious mind or of a different reality of mind awareness, which is an extrasensory state of consciousness. They are both categorized as illusions because they cannot be reached by waking consciousness.

The events that occur in our dreams cause all sorts of feelings and emotions in us. They are very similar to the experiences we have when we are awake, as they are both products of our minds. Both experiences cause the same bodily effects on us, although they belong to different types and levels of mind awareness.

Extra Sensory Perception (ESP)

Extrasensory perception is a term used by Duke University psychologist Joseph Banks Rhine. It refers to information received not through our five physical senses but sensed directly through our mind (Mauskopf, Seymour, McVaugh, Michael 1981, vol.36-3, 310-311).

Our mind has telepathic qualities that can seriously affect our life. It is constantly sending and receiving energies. Our unconscious mind is linked to the unconscious mind of all beings everywhere through the medium of the one Universal Mind, or the Mind of God.

Whatever we think or feel during every moment of our lives gets telepathically broadcast to every single existence on Earth and beyond.

Although the people we think of are not aware of our thoughts or feelings on a conscious level, they may be able to sense telepathically the general trend of our thinking. They may get favourably or unfavourably affected by us, depending on the nature of our thoughts or feelings towards them.

Based on the law of attraction, like attracts like. Transmitted thoughts and emotional energies of goodness, health, confidence, success, love, and health attract to us just the same positive energies. The same happens with the negative energies too.

Based on the above, we should take a few moments, every day to send good and godly thoughts to everyone we know, and even better, to all of humanity at large, so that we may receive goodness back in return.

It seems that physical laws can be altered by our minds. We can influence reality and manifest anything we want directly out of the interaction of the quantum field energy that surrounds us. There are fewer chances, though, to experience ESP events when we live in our past rather than live in the present, because living in our past renders us incapable of recognizing these appearances in our lives.

Evidence of ESP

Increasing evidence is demonstrating that ESP does exist, but it cannot be explained or quantified by physical laws. Many of us have experienced, the so-called unusual phenomena like dreams that come true, meaningful unexpected coincidences, miraculous unexplained cases of healing, near-death and out-of-body experiences. These types of events fall outside the realm of human or even scientific comprehension based on the means that are available to us at this point in time.

In fact, what we humans can perceive with our naked eye is extremely limited. The human visible spectrum goes only from 380 to 770 nanometres. This means that humans are only capable of perceiving one octave of light of this entire light spectrum. The fact that we cannot see the rest of the spectrum does not mean that it is not there. It means that our five senses are very limited to what we can perceive. Therefore, there is a strong possibility that there is far more out there than what humanity's sophisticated technology can discover right now. Perhaps there are hidden dimensions, other universes, and alternate unseen worlds that exist right next to our own.

Synchronicity

The term "synchronicity," was used initially by the Swiss psychiatrist and psychoanalyst Jung. It is used to describe coincidental, simultaneous, or meaningful events that many people have experienced in their lives but to which they have not given much credit.

Jung has described synchronicities as "temporally coincident occurrences of acausal events" and also as "meaningful coincidences" or as an "acausal connecting principle" or as an "acausal parallelism" (Jung 2021).

Nothing can happen out of mere chance in a universe in which there is so much law and order. Based on the order of the universe and on our interaction with the Universal Intelligence, synchronicities seem to be well-orchestrated events in our life, coordinated by the Universal Mind. They seem to be acts synchronized by a higher intelligence that operates in our world. These synchronized events create an invisible bridge that starts in our outer world and it connects us with our inner realities and with the consciousness of other living creatures.

My Personal Experiences

I believe very strongly in the occurrence of miracles. I have experienced too many miracles and positive, meaningful coincidences, which have affected my life in many ways, to think otherwise.

Here are some of my personal experiences of synchronicity. When my mother was at her mid-sixties, she tripped on the carpet in our home, fell down and she hurt her upper back. The next day, she saw her doctor, who ordered X-rays. When they looked at the X-rays, they realized that the there was no fracture caused by the fall, but there was a growth in her thyroid gland. When they tested the growth, they found out that it was malignant. Consequently, they operated on her and removed the tumour. If it was not for the fall, who knows when they would have found out about the cancerous growth.

Few years ago, on a Friday afternoon, I was coming home from church. At one intersection, in the downtown Vancouver area, I saw a woman who was looking for spare change. I stopped, I pulled over, searched inside my purse, I found few pieces of silver, and I gave them to her. This incident must have taken me about one or two minutes. I then proceeded towards Stanley Park on my way to the North Shore. As I was driving through the park and just before crossing the bridge, a huge tree fell onto to the car which was three cars ahead of me. Luckily, they were not casualties, just damage to the car's bonnet and windscreen. That tree would have definitely fallen on my car if that lady had not stopped me asking for alms...

For me personally, when I have experiences of synchronicity with positive outcomes to any problem, I consider those as the best possible proof of the oneness of the universe and of the existence of Universal Intelligence that controls and guides us.

These beliefs give me a sense of identity, purpose, connectivity, power, and meaning in my life. They reassure me that our purpose in this life is to expand our conscious awareness and to live as spiritual beings, connected to our Creator.

Synchronized Events

Synchronized events make some people believe that we are all interconnected through an invisible spiritual web, that coordinates our lives and makes us who we are, in this energy and matter filled whole, we call the Universe.

Unexpected coincidences and circumstances often connect people who have not met before and who may never have met each other, in their lifetimes. These interconnections based on the principle of "synchronicity" often make a great difference in the lives of total strangers.

When we experience a profound case of synchronicity, we should remember that we live in an intelligent, multidimensional Universe in which a case of synchronicity is more than just a coincidence. It is a proof that our inner and outer worlds are somehow connected and that we are guided by the power of the universe.

Although the source of this immeasurable coordinating Universal Power, or God may be invisible to us and undetectable by our five senses, the faithful observer can experience its effects in many ways. These effects can be acknowledged either as an act of kindness or love by a fellow human being or even as an opportunity that is unexpectedly presented to us. They normally create significant changes in our life in the form of guidance as a result of prayer.

It is amazing to observe how our whole body reacts to acts of synchronicity, which when they are correctly identified, recognized, and interpreted in our daily activities, do tend to increase our sense of expanded consciousness. They make us realize that we are both physical and spiritual beings, and that our purpose in life is both physical and spiritual.

Einstein once said,

> A human being is a part of a whole, called Universe, a part limited in time and space. He experiences himself, his thoughts and feelings as something separated from the rest... a kind of optical delusion of his consciousness. This delusion is a kind of prison for us, restricting us to our personal desires and to affection for a few persons nearest to us. Our task must be to free ourselves from this prison by widening our circle of compassion to embrace all living creatures and the whole of nature in its beauty. (Myss 2006, 53)

Warren Weaver, a well-known mathematician, wrote the following unbelievable story in his book *Lady Luck: The Theory of Probability*. No rational thinking could explain this, and it is a proof of synchronicity. He mentioned that fifteen members of a church choir in Beatrice, Nebraska, were supposed to be in church at 7:20p.m. for a rehearsal on the 1st of March, 1950. None of the fifteen arrived on time. Somehow, they all had their own personal, ordinary, unconnected reasons for being late for the rehearsal.

Eventually it was considered that the delay of the members of the choir was rather extremely fortunate and "an act of God," as at 7:25p.m. the church building was completely destroyed in an explosion. Weaver calculated the staggering odds against chance for this uncanny event to be about one chance in a million (Weaver 1982).

When Jung was developing his synchronicity theory, he was obviously influenced by the increased popularity of the concept of synchronicity and the role of consciousness in the physical world. He believed that matter and consciousness are interconnected and function together, complimenting each other. Based on his research of the collective unconscious during his career as a psychiatrist, he also believed that the cases of meaningful coincidences to which he was exposed, were beyond the mathematical calculation of probabilities.

Intuition

Intuition is the ability to understand something from instinctive feeling rather than from conscious reasoning. These instinctive feelings are generated in our minds and in our individual electromagnetic energy fields, which contain information that gets constantly transmitted and received from us and from others.

Certain people have the ability to detect codes that come from higher realms of reality. These are the God-inspired intuitions that can be realized through the higher frequencies which cause the higher vibratory rate of our consciousness.

The higher vibration frequencies can be achieved through meditation and through the practice of virtuous acts as for example, acts of gratitude, love, generosity, forgiveness, and compassion.

When these higher vibrations harmonize with even higher rates of vibrations in the Universe, they give us access to the universal realm of knowledge.

Applications of ESP

The following is a very interesting story on how the U.S. government has used the human ability of extrasensory perception:

> During the tense period of the Cold War, the US government sought to deploy a potent new weapon against the Soviet Union: mind-reading. In a highly classified project conducted first in a California research lab in the 1970s, and later at an Army base in Maryland, the CIA, Army and Defense Intelligence Agency recruited men and women claiming to have powers of extrasensory perception (ESP) to help uncover military and domestic intelligence secrets. In 2017, the CIA declassified some 12 million pages of records revealing previously unknown details about the program, which would eventually become known as Project Star Gate. By the time the program was shut down in 1995, psychics known as "remote viewers" had taken part in a wide array of operations, from locating hostages kidnapped by Islamic terrorist groups to tracing the paths of fugitive criminals within the United States.

The roots of Project Star Gate go back to 1972, when a classified report made waves within the U.S. military and intelligence communities by claiming that the Soviet Union was pouring money into research involving ESP and psychokinesis—the ability to move objects with the mind—for espionage purposes. In response, the CIA began funding its own top-secret research, headquartered at the Stanford Research Institute in Menlo Park, California (Pruitt 2018).

ESP Connections

When we make a spiritual, extrasensory connection with another person, we feel the essence of God within that individual. The nineteenth century Swiss psychiatrist and psychoanalyst Carl Jung, who founded analytical psychology, stated that "the meeting of two personalities is like the contact of two chemical substances; if there is any reaction, both are transformed" (Jung 2010, 57).

This exact same thing takes place when we meditate on God's presence daily. Our meditation acts as a power source that gives greater energy to our transmitted thoughts and feelings.

Classic rationalists are not prepared to consider anything that defies logic or anything that exists beyond the known borders of human consciousness. Many influential thinkers of the past, though-many philosophers, advanced spiritual leaders, and even scientists with expanded consciousness-have recognized and experienced events that fall outside the borders of the current scientific thought. They have talked about them and they have analyzed the underlying truths that exist between belief and skepticism.

Our scientists are already working on the idea of placing a computer chip inside the human body for a better communication and control on the individual people. So why it is impossible for an inborn communication system to exist within the whole creation?

If the above sounds somehow plausible, we may have an inborn ability within us which acts as a type of a universal transmitter and receiver between the human mind and the Mind of God. The possibility of this connection would enable us to receive guidance from the Creator, which will be for our benefit and for the improvement of the way we live. Our ability to transmit our every wish and thought through specific energy frequencies in our body and mind would help make this connection easier. The amount of guidance we receive would be directly proportional to the oneness we feel to the consciousness of God within our mind.

CHAPTER FOUR

"If you wish to understand the secrets of the universe, think of energy, frequency, and vibration."

Dr. Nikola Tesla 1942

ENERGY

Everything in our world is made up of energy, which can be changed from one form to another but cannot be destroyed based on the law of thermodynamics. Our whole Universe is made up of energy. All things are constantly in motion, vibrating in different frequencies.

Although, everything in the Universe, seems to be solid, including the very Earth upon which we stand, no object is truly solid. Everything is an energy field that vibrates in a regular, periodic manner. There is nothing in the Universe that does not vibrate. The famous German-born theoretical physicist of the nineteenth century, Albert Einstein, said, "Everything in life is vibration" (Dabhi 2021, YouTube).

Our Cosmos is an energy web, which emanates life force to all its entities. They continually receive and transmit energy. Every creation in the Universe is a manifestation of this Universal energy, which is part of everything that exists. All living creatures are biological units of energy; life itself is an interaction of various energy fields. This interaction of energies causes the enormous influence of the mind upon the body. The human mind is a field of energy that utilizes brain cells to function. Emotions and feelings are also energies. We humans are representatives of the energy of divine love in a human form.

We create our own energy field by the way we treat ourselves inside and out. Thus, we are responsible for our energy field and all our life experiences. The degree that we receive and transmit physical, spiritual, and psychic higher energy is in direct relation to the extent of our spiritual development. The more spiritually evolved we are, the higher energy frequencies we emit. These higher frequencies attune better with cosmic energy frequencies, which act like magnets attracting positive experiences in our lives.

The more individuals subscribe to separateness by choosing actions that they think only benefit or hurt themselves, the more we will all suffer. The more individuals live toward oneness for the good of the whole, the more we will all be lifted up.

Starve your soul of hate, anger, fear, greed, blame, and judgment. Feed your soul with unconditional love for all your humanity and the world will be a better place for all.

There is only peace in oneness and only love in such a state of oneness.

Divine Energy

Our Universe has an amazing intelligent design, which is filled by an invisible divine energy that connects all the living creatures within it. We all share the same energy that emanates from the same one source.

The divine energy within us is not our own separate spark of God. It belongs to the Universe. We are simply borrowing it for a while in order to exist as a part of the whole on this Earth, in the same way that we are borrowing from this Earth all the elements that exist in our bodies.

We are all an extension of this universe, this galaxy and this earth. This extension of us, which is our natural state of being is a stage of oneness with everything and everyone.

Psychic Energy

Energy comes from a single source, which emanates an interacting life force to all its entities in the Universe. It is holographic, vibrating and moving continuously. It cannot be created or destroyed but it can only change form (Einstein, $E=MC^2$).

This one source of energy, which in Christianity we call "the Holy Spirit" and in Hinduism "the Atman" is the life-giving Spirit of God. Life is a flow of energy directed by God. It flows through all living things, and it dominates everything. It guides and sustains us continually and interacts with each one of us constantly. When we experience the power of this life-giving energy, our ability of making changes to ourselves and to others gets initiated and increases. We learn to live not *at* each other, not *with* each other, but *for* each other.

The main cause of both positive and negative psychic energy, which fills the atmosphere in numerous locations on this planet, comes from the energies of humankind. When the energy is positive, it affects positively all the energy fields of our body and mind, and we get pleasure from being a part of it. If the energy is negative, we experience health destroying effects brought about by the pressure of the negative energies in the body. It is important to remember that negative energy has far less power to affect us if positive, higher consciousness energy is present in our body and mind.

Raise the energy consciousness of both your body and mind to the positive energy of higher consciousness. Meditate daily on God's presence, in order to eliminate the negative energies that work against you.

Thought Energy

Our thoughts are made up of exactly the same vibrational energy that exists in nature. They are the forces with which we build our world. They are the creative building material which shape our past, present, and future lives according to their nature.

Man transmits energy with his mind. Every thought is a transmitted energy. All thoughts originate in the person's mind and as such, they are subject to change.

We do continuously send various thought vibrations of different frequencies to others around us, and we receive various thought vibrations from them. Those different frequencies depend on our various emotional, mental and spiritual states of consciousness.

The extent of our physical, spiritual, and psychic transmission and reception of higher energy is in direct relation to our mental and spiritual development and to the degree of our tuning to the cosmic energy frequencies. We are responsible for the type of energy we transmit, on which most of our good or bad life experiences depend. Our transmitted energy field acts like a magnet, attracting the same sort of experiences that match our field.

We are the creators of our life circumstances and of our future. Our thinking has created the world we live in, at the present time. Frederick Lenz, an American contemporary spiritual teacher, said, "All physical and nonphysical things have another side, a side that is not visible to the senses or accessible to the reasoning mind, a side that can only be known and experienced intuitively by emptying one's own mind of thoughts" (Lewinson- Lenz 2020).

Our mind is also creating the duality on the basis of which we make our classifications and base our beliefs. This duality makes the split between the self and other, mine and yours, man and nature, inner and outer, good or bad, and so on.

Effects Of Thought Energy

Problems are created as direct results of thought energies in our mind, and they are considered temporary even if they last for years.

Life is perceived not as a series of events but as a series of experiences. Experiences start as thoughts in our minds and then become actions. Therefore, if we control our thoughts, we will be controlling our attitudes, our actions, our experiences, and subsequently the quality of our lives. By controlling our thoughts, our actions, and our imagination, we become the masters of our destiny, liberated from suffering.

When the energies we send and receive are out of balance then our physical and mental health get affected in one way or another causing most of our earthly problems. If we do not learn how to control our thoughts, we become products and prisoners of our own minds and of the world surrounding us. The quality of our life is a function of the quality of our thoughts and of our level of awareness.

Our thoughts create our emotions, which affect our physical body, our nervous system, and our endocrine system. They affect our energy, our real self, our spirit, and our soul. This means that they affect us physically, psychologically, and spiritually. U. S. Andersen, a successful self-help author in the 1950s and 1960s, said, "Nothing is impossible to the mind. All its guidance and power are available to you. When you fully realize that thought causes all, you will know there are never any limits that you yourself do not impose" (Andersen 2020, quote 923788).

We can change the quality of our thoughts positively when we apply the greater divine energy to them. We do that by sinking into our innermost self and feel the presence of God in the centre of our mind. When we contact God within ourselves, the divine power inside us overpowers all the lesser negative energies, which change or disappear.

Negative thoughts only have an effect on us when we react to them. If we can classify any thought as desirable or undesirable and hold on to positive thoughts only, we will be able to see what we want to see in our lives.

If we realize how powerful our thoughts are, we will never allow a negative thought to pass through our mind.

One man was travelling and suddenly he got to paradise. He sat down under the desire tree (there is such tree in paradise, sitting under which you can immediately fulfill any desire, you just need to think about it) and thought: 'I am hungry, so it would be nice to have a bite right now.' And when he just thought about this, a table full of different dishes that he was thinking about appeared right before him. 'Wow!' – The man was surprised, – 'but it can't be!' – He thought so, and the table with dishes disappeared immediately. 'It would be nice to get it back!' – And dishes appeared again. He ate a plenty of dishes – he has never eaten such tasty food before. After satisfying hunger he thought: 'It would be nice to drink something' – and a perfect wine appeared immediately, because there are no restrictions in the paradise. Lying in the shadow of the tree and drinking wine, he started wondering: 'Why do these miracles happen? It just can't be that everything would be so good – probably some ghosts played a joke on me.' Suddenly the ghosts appeared. They were terrible and looked like he imagined them. The man became scared and thought: 'Now they will kill me!' And they killed him. Everyone lives in the world that he deserved. (Anonymous)

Facing Problems

Encountering problems and challenges in life is inevitable, no matter how much we try to avoid them by controlling our thoughts and our behaviour.

Life is a journey and each stage is a level we must go through and learn from. Each learning process is transformative. The outcome is irrelevant; what matters is what we have learned from it and how we have evolved through it.

We should not complain about the bad things we encounter every day and about all kinds of malicious and inconsiderate people we may come into contact with. Instead, we should build ourselves up to become a superior, noble person and go towards our goals without complaining about our limitations.

The positive point about suffering and facing problems in life is that they make us stronger and transcend us if we know what to learn from them. The biggest lessons we learn come from our biggest tragedies because they make us face our biggest fears, our biggest vulnerabilities and our biggest desires.

Try and think of the most painful episodes you have lived; think of the vulnerabilities they revealed in you. Why have you suffered? What illusions about life or people have you lost? Accept the loss, no matter how painful, and try to see the episodes as an observer. What knowledge have you gained by losing some of your illusions? How can this knowledge help you in case you are faced with similar events?

Whatever does not destroy us mentally, physically, and psychologically makes us stronger, as long as we remain alive and capable of learning. We need to be like Phoenix, always ready to rise up from the abyss and from our ashes. To evolve, we must sometimes destroy our old selves in some way to rise anew and be stronger and wiser.

We do not need to solve our problems by ourselves. Instead, we need to rise to a higher level of consciousness and view the problem from a higher point of mind. Solving problems in the world by ourselves gives us only a momentary and a temporary high, until an empty space gets created inside us, for the next problem to appear.

Instead of trying to live this life alone, relying only on the power of our intellect and on our personal abilities, let us rather confirm to ourselves our oneness with God's presence and spirit. Let us stay positive even when situations in our lives are not good and easy. Let us remember and try, through prayer and faith, to access the deeper dimensions of spirituality, through which we can receive direction, assistance, and protection from God.

When we turn over our problems to the Universal Mind of God, we turn them over to the ultimate, absolute, most powerful presence in the Universe. We are able to transcend the difficult situation through the power of God and find a permanent solution granting us freedom, control and happiness. God's eternal power is greater than any temporary problem we may be having or will ever have.

Positive visualizations of ideal states of being, lead to a wonderful adventure through life in which we have full control and mastery of what is happening to us and around us. Changing our life experience is not about changing the world around us, but changing our thoughts and our perception of the world.

PART THREE

The Emotional Aspect

"Do not dwell in the past, do not dream of the future,
concentrate the mind on the present moment."
Buddha

CHAPTER FIVE

"I don't want to be at the mercy of my emotions. I want
to use them, to enjoy them, and to dominate them."
Oscar Wilde

FEELINGS AND EMOTIONS

Feelings and emotions are products of our thoughts. They
affect our physical body, our nervous system, and our endocrine system. They affect our energy, our spirit, and our soul.
This means that they affect us physically, psychologically,
and spiritually.

It is a proven scientific fact that projecting positive energy
of loving thoughts towards humans, animals, or even plants
make a big difference in our lives. Experiments have shown
that even plants towards which positive energy of love has
been projected thrive much better compared to plants that
receive no energy or that receive negative energy.

Thoughts of anger, fear, and anxiety produce changes in the chemistry of the brain, which cause detrimental effects in the physiology of our body and initiate the onset of disease.

Any form of help and assistance offered or received consciously by love, personal attention, and compassion becomes a catalyst for a chain reaction to start. It initiates an act of power and healing, through which we transfer energy or grace to each other. Emotions of generosity, empathy, and compassion towards others, irrespective of whether they are friends, co-workers, or strangers, have positive effects on our healthy emotional and social growth. They make us feel happier by activating pleasure circuits in our brains and by lowering our stress levels.

By doing more unselfish acts of kindness, by spreading unselfish, unconditional love, we send a message to the natural healing intelligence inside our mind to open the channels of divine energy. Thus, a healing process starts in our inner and outer selves as well as in the people around us.

Positive, kind emotions also strengthen our immune system; reduce the risk of heart attacks and the negative effects of loneliness.

Research in the Northern Arizona University has shown that compassion

- makes us happy by activating pleasure circuits in our brain,
- lowers our stress levels,
- strengthens our immune system,
- reduces the risk of heart attacks,

- reduces the negative effects of loneliness
  (https://in.nau.edu/eaw/september-is-all-about-
  kindness-and-compassion-at-eaw).

Thomas Merton, a contemporary American monk, writer, theologian, and mystic, taught, "Therefore the man who loves himself too much is incapable of loving anyone effectively, including himself. How then can he hope to love another" (Merton 2002, 11).

A personality- and ego- driven love, only isolates us from others and makes us care about ourselves only. Love that emanates from our higher, real self and our enlightened consciousness is what makes us live for others, love others, give to others, share with others, and feel one with the rest of humanity and creation, in general.

Emotional Intelligence
The term "emotional intelligence" was created by two researchers, Peter Salavoy and John Mayer, in their article "Emotional Intelligence" in the journal Imagination, Cognition and Personality in 1990 (Salavoy- Mayer 1990, Vol 9, 3).

We define emotional intelligence (or EI) as the ability to recognize, understand, and manage our own emotions and recognize, understand, and influence the emotions of others. In practical terms, this means being aware of the fact that our emotions can drive our behaviour and impact people positively and negatively. It means learning how to manage those emotions.

DISCOVER THE ETERNAL YOU!

It's a scientific fact that emotions precede thought, and so they do change the way our brain functions. Emotions can diminish our cognitive abilities, our decision-making powers, and even interpersonal skills. Understanding and managing our emotions helps us to think more clearly. It causes us to be more successful in our personal and professional lives by avoiding uncomfortable conversations that hurt feelings.

Happiness

Happiness is a state of mind; therefore, it can only be found inside us. It is wrong to look for happiness outside ourselves. We decide if we want to be happy or not. No external circumstances or other people can be the cause of our happiness or unhappiness. People are as happy as they make up their minds to be.

Happiness is not the goal of life but the aim in life. It is not necessarily linked to feelings of pleasure, joy, or ecstasy. In reality, happiness is a matter of choice and decision. It can only be achieved by removing suffering, controlling our mind, keeping a check on our needs, and eliminating our desires.

My Friend's Story

When my friend lost her only grandson to a motorbike accident, I thought that she would never recover from the shock and the pain she felt. It seemed that her life had come to a halt. She lost her sense of being, her ideals changed, her faith was shaken. She became depressed and felt very sorry for herself. She felt that her grief and pain would never subside. She spent the first couple years following his death, in solitude and in denial of what had happened. She had difficult times since her youth, but the pain of the loss of a grandchild was unsurpassable, she thought.

After counselling her for two years and trying to help her with her suicidal moods, suddenly something changed. Something happened that I didn't foresee. One day she made the choice to be happy. She decided to live each day as happy as she could by being positive and trying to avoid any negative thoughts and emotions. She practised redirecting and forcing her thoughts to things she loved like favourite dishes, peaceful music, loving pets, pleasant films.

Of course, it was very hard in the beginning, and the effort was immense, but slowly, her brain got trained to avoid any negative thought passing by. She was determined to be happy, and she was making a conscious effort to achieve it. In just a matter of a few weeks, I saw an immense change in her. She had found her old self…

She had decided that happiness is a choice, and until one goes through the process of forcing oneself to be happy, life will be miserable and lonely. She accepted the fact that "this is life", and the world with all its ups and downs, is still a good place.

Her transformation was worth all the efforts.

Striving For Happiness

People have always wondered if lasting happiness is possible. The fact is that the majority of people never experienced lasting happiness because most of them are living self-centred and self-interested lives. They are trying to find happiness through outside sources, such as another person, material wealth, fame, and power, missing the point that love and compassion are the bases of permanent happiness.

We all strive for happiness but we have a special talent for making ourselves miserable. Normally we are not aware of how happy we are until we start to experience a certain degree of emotional suffering.

We seem to think that if we acquire certain things, visit some places, and meet the right person, then we will be happy, but that is a delusion. Suffering will always pursue us, although the things that cause us pain may change with time or with changing outer conditions and circumstances. In other words, the focus of pain may change, but not the actual pain and suffering as such. Even if there is nothing to cause us pain, boredom will make us suffer.

In order to be happy, we need to remember the happy times we had in life, to evaluate where we are now and what kind of suffering, we are experiencing, and make the effort to remove it. By remembering our happy moments and trying to relive them as much as possible, we experience feelings of happiness again.

Compassion towards other human beings gives meaning to our existence, and meaning leads to happiness. Greek philosopher Plato identified happiness with spiritual well-being, with a state of harmony in the soul and with an inner peace that results from the proper order of all the soul's parts, namely the rational, the spirited, and the appetitive parts. He believed that thinking with compassion and doing things for others while abandoning the personal ego self is the basic foundation for living a meaningful and fulfilling life and experiencing lasting happiness.

In addition to compassion, a moral life is a much happier life than a life led by personal desires and by goal chasings. In fact, the Greek philosopher Socrates wrote in his book *The Republic* that the just man will be happier than the unjust, even if by all the external considerations, he seems to be at a disadvantage.

Do not hurt anyone but help everyone, as much as you can; after all, we are all in this life together. Think well before you speak and act; be fair and considerate towards all; help the ones that need your help.

Avoid holding resentments and anger. They are poisons to our souls, and they consume us deeply. It is the sign of weakness and of a slave mentality in a person. They harm no one other than the person who holds them. Take the necessary immediate steps to remedy any situation, and afterwards forget, forgive, and move on.

A strong person is able to forget and recover. He does not hold on to the memory of a painful situation for very long, and he does not let that affect his peace of mind.

Unhappiness

Our entire life is nothing more than a bundle of thoughts, of feelings, of emotions, and experiences rather than events. When a continuous flow of often-painful thoughts flood through our mind, the effect of these thoughts in our life and health become disastrous.

According to quantum physics everything we perceive is a thought, which creates waves that travel around the world and they can influence the whole Universe.

The two main reasons of unhappiness in life are pain and boredom, which prevent us from having a fulfilled life. Boredom is the state when we have everything, we need but we are not satisfied with anything.

The solution is to depend less on the outside world, less on possession, less on success, less on fame, and more on our self. We need to concentrate more on our body, mind and inner life and have a more holistic approach to life. We need to be aware of each moment and of the more essential things in life, like our breath and our blessings.

According to the law of attraction, when we think of something that we really wish for, when we focus our full attention on it, and when we charge it with the appropriate vibrating energy of feelings and emotion, then we create a magnetic field that attracts to us everything in the Universe that is in harmony with our thoughts.

Our state of mind causes the state of synthesis, harmony and balance between our body, mind and spirit. This is what makes us feel whole and complete and gives both meaning and fulfillment to our life. Therefore, by entertaining more uplifting thoughts, we can choose to enjoy life fully.

We may not be able to control what is happening in the world around us, but we can definitely control fully how we handle each situation and what types of emotions we produce. No negative emotion can be produced by external causes or by what life throws at us.

Art and Happiness

Art and music are sources of happiness in our life. Art has the quality to transcend reality and to connect us with the real spiritual essence of the world. By listening to high quality music, contemplating the beauty of a painting or sculpture, and photographing beautiful landscapes and sunsets, we help elevate our souls, escape from the ordinary, temporary life, and liberate ourselves from the ordinary desires and needs.

Music is the best way to see the true essence of the world. Scientists in Stanford University did lots of studies on the Baroque music of the eighteenth century, and it was proven that when we listen to Baroque music, as well as most pieces of classical music, the level of awareness and intelligence in our brain increases.

A Nashville Journalist by the name of Jordan Taylor Sloan, claims that not only does pop music have negative effects on our brains, but pop music fans are likely to be less creative than any other kind of music lover (Sloan 2014).

CHAPTER SIX

"The greatest virtues are those which are
most useful to other persons."
Aristotle

VIRTUES

I remember reading once, that the nineteenth-century German philosopher, cultural critic and philologist Nietzsche considered virtue to be a type of altruistic behaviour which focuses on the good of others, rather than the self.

A virtue is a complex disposition which is concerned with such things as desires, thoughts, actions, emotions, and feelings. It means showing behaviour of what is considered to be of high moral standards and of what is ethical, right and good. It implies moral excellence in character.

Aristotle, the famous Greek philosopher and polymath during the classical period in Ancient Greece, believed that virtue is in man by nature and not acquired during his life. He thought that one had to demonstrate his virtuous nature by acting for good ends. Socrates, on the other hand, believed that man is not virtuous by nature. One learns to be virtuous as "virtue is knowledge", he claimed. Through learning about virtue and behaving in a virtuous manner, we can live our life in the best possible manner.

Although the emotional aspect of virtues has been long neglected and too much importance has been attached to the rational aspect of them, emotions constitute the fundamental basis of virtues as they supply the intention to their formation.

Some examples of virtues are honesty, courage, humility, modesty, compassion, generosity, fidelity, patience, integrity, self-control, prudence, and wisdom.

A very good example of living a most virtuous life is Mother Teresa, or Saint Teresa of Calcutta, an Albanian-Indian Roman Catholic nun, of the twentieth century, born in Skopje. She lived and worked in India for seventeen years. In 1950 she founded the order of the Missionaries of Charity, which she was an active member of. She was a Nobel Peace Prize winner.

Mother Teresa, dedicated her life to caring for the destitute and dying in the slums of Calcutta. She demonstrated unconditional love for humanity with prudence and wisdom. She acted with great humility for the unbelievable work she achieved.

Her unlimited compassion for the poor, the suffering, the ill, and the dying is a great example of selfless dedication and of love for God through charity.

If we live our lives with values like integrity, charity, love, selflessness and compassion, we will be blessed with positive energy and fulfillment.

PART FOUR

The Spiritual Aspect

"Science is not only compatible with spirituality;
it is a profound source of spirituality."

Carl Sagan

CHAPTER SEVEN

"We are not human beings having a spiritual experience.
We are spiritual beings having a human experience."
Pierre Teilhard de Chardin

SPIRITUALITY

Spirituality is the term we use for the belief of the indestructibility of our energy essence, our spirit, or our soul.

The essence of all spiritual practices is to acknowledge the infinite power within us and the effort to engage with it. It is about leaving our mind totally open to the Divine Mind so that our higher consciousness takes over our human consciousness and it works through us.

Spirituality is based on the acceptance of
- the existence of a higher omnipotent intelligence in the Universe,
- the presence of other higher dimensions than the one we are experiencing through our five senses and,

- the possibility of attaining higher levels of consciousness or conscious awareness through which we can access what lies beyond our physical reality.

There's a great search in our world today for a new type of spirituality. People are looking to achieve a new type of relationship with God. They are realizing that knowledge alone will not improve and elevate the quality of one's life unless spirituality is applied to daily living. Obviously, knowledge has to be obtained first, and then its application to life's pursuits must follow. Without such application, spiritual truths have no practical value, either in physical life or spiritually.

Spiritual Development

Spiritual development focuses on the maturity of our spiritual nature and on the notion of the existence of God's spirit in our hearts. Carl Jung described spiritual maturity as an awakening to the need to live a life of spiritual purpose, rather than a life simply fulfilling the basic needs of physical survival or the pursuit of pleasure (Myss 2006, 6).

We can devote more time to our spiritual awakening in order to enhance our spiritual progress

- by using the metaphysical tools of faith, prayer, and meditation daily,
- by practising humility, charity, morality, and goodness,
- by living consciously, and
- by being connected to our inner self, or our soul.

We all make progress according to our own individual requirements until we reach the state of personal fulfillment, of profound peace, and of internal happiness, and until every aspect of our life gets positively affected.

What Does Spirituality Offer us?

When we achieve spiritual awakening and spiritual enlightenment, we experience the mystical reality of the expanded states of consciousness. We get to know and understand that our higher, true self is part of the divine creation, and we feel a oneness with the Universe and with all the creatures in it.

Spirituality provides us with

- a deeper understanding of the concept of God,
- a life filled with purpose and excitement as we connect with the wonder and power of the divine,
- compassion, empathy, strength and courage,
- a highly evolved state of unselfishness and humility as we become conduits for the divine and
- spontaneity, transparency, and accessibility to the divine.

People who are spiritually awakened handle their life problems and difficulties with inner strength and hope. They look at the trials of life with a spiritual approach and derive strength from the divine energy they access. They know that they are not just passive observers of life but active participants in is events.

Without spiritual development, one has no mastery over one's life, no guidance, and no direction. One is like a boat left without oars, an engine, or sails in the middle of an ocean.

Absence of Spirituality

Everything in our earthly life is ideas and speculations, imagination, and beliefs, all of which are weak and change-able. Life is full of distractions that keep us from focusing on God and on our spiritual life. We need to pause for a while, focus on our lives and listen to our inner voice.

If we live in untruth, we are separated from God. God is at a distance or God is nowhere at all. If we cannot experience God in our lives, we do not feel the divine light. This means that our egos have taken over; it means that our distance from our real selves and from our God has widened up and that our connection has been broken down. Consequently, our prayers do not get answered, and we live a life of struggle and misfortune. When we fight the will of God, nothing happens; everything comes to a standstill.

We need to strive to get inner inspiration instead of just stimulation and excitement on the outside. This is what will give real purpose to our intellect and will enable us to get in touch with the wisdom within in order to seek guidance in our decision-making and freedom from ambivalence and confusion.

Transcending Physical Reality

Many people go through life with limitations which they place upon themselves, while others have risen above such conditions and transcended this reality in order to have fuller and more complete lives.

How can we transcend this physical reality? How can we leave the problems associated with this physical dimension behind? And how can we enjoy the bliss associated with transcendence?

We can achieve transcendence by possessing faith, praising God, meditating, and praying unceasingly. Mark the Evangelist, also known as Saint Mark, quoted Jesus when he said, "So I tell you, whatever you ask for in prayer, believe that you have received it, and it will be yours" (Mark, 11:24).

Also, we can achieve transcendence by evangelizing, practising humility and righteousness, and doing benevolent deeds by loving and forgiving. John the evangelist and beloved friend of Jesus quotes, "Whoever does not love, does not know God"(1 John: 8). Our basic need to give and receive love comes from the divine part in us.

The stronger our spiritual focus is the higher our state of consciousness will be, the better our inner contact with God will be, and the more successful our outer focus will be in improving our life.

Importance of Humility in Spirituality

"What I see in Nature is a magnificent structure
that we can comprehend only very imperfectly,
and that must fill a thinking person with a feeling
of humility. This is a genuinely religious feeling
that has nothing to do with mysticism."
Albert Einstein

Humility is the foundation of spirituality. It is the most important attribute and quality of character for a successful spiritual life. It is a necessary part of the path to enlightenment and holiness as it enables us to attune our mind to the Mind of God. Without humility, there can be no spiritual progress.

Humility is a major theme in both the Old and New Testaments. It is the concept of abandoning one's thoughts of grandeur, self-power, and "me-first" thinking. It offers emotional autonomy and freedom from social control and the *established sense of self.*

Humility not only paves the way to God's guidance and presence in one's life but it requires the development of virtues such as sincerity, honesty, and genuine self-criticism in people. "The simple-hearted, patient people who humbly trust their heavenly Father and have confidence in Him rather than their own thoughts, power, and control attract the grace of God"(Proverbs, 22:4).

A well-developed sense of humility shines through in our behaviour toward others as we make everyone around us feel appreciated, encouraged, and validated.

The Spiritual Property of Food

Food is generally considered to be a means of physical sustenance, and it is therefore viewed in its purely chemical aspect. We believe that the food we eat is solely for the maintenance of the chemical and physical constitution of the body and for vitality.

When we start to realize that man is not just a mere physical body and that he has two divisions in his being; namely the physiochemical constitution and the spiritual side, we will understand that we are not only dependent upon the chemical elements in the food eaten.

Our spiritual side is surely dependent upon the physical body and its condition. Our body is an instrument by which our intellect and the divine attributes we possess become manifest. If we practice healthy eating, our bodies and minds will be better attuned to higher frequencies. They will be better prepared to function as conduits for the extremely healing energies of the higher frequencies.

There are several ways in which spirituality enters our physical body. One is through the air we breathe; another is from the sun; another through nature; and another through the quality of the foods we eat and drink.

Proper breathing, regular exercising; and eating vital foods are extremely beneficial for a healthy body and a healthy mind. Vital foods consist of vegetables, green leaves, stems, and branches that rise above the surface of the Earth. Thus, they receive plenty of moisture and sun and are filled with a large amount of spiritual energy, which is essential for the development of the spiritual side of life.

CHAPTER EIGHT

"If we could see the miracle of a single flower
clearly, our whole life would change."
Buddha

MIRACLES

A miracle is defined as *"an event that is inexplicable by natural
or scientific laws and accordingly gets attributed to some supernatural or preternatural cause."* (https://en.wikipedia.org/
wiki/Miracle)

Miracles are meant to prove God's power, which alters
physical laws and makes a difference in our lives. They are
most probably products of some unseen cause and effect that
have been in progress for a very long time.

Research in quantum physics points to the existence of
a nonmaterial Universe and to an extrasensory force that
exists in another reality and intersects and integrates with
the physical world.

I am strongly convinced that any form of help and assistance we offer or receive consciously by love and by compassion is an act of power and healing. Through those virtuous acts, we transfer energy or grace to each other.

Author and alternative medicine advocate Deepak Chopra in his book, *How to know God,* that "Everything that we experience as material reality is born in an invisible realm beyond space and time, a realm revealed by science to consist of energy and information." Chopra reckons that something creates and organizes this chaotic energy and turns it into stars, galaxies, forests, humans, emotions, and memories. He believes that it is not only possible to know this source of existence on an abstract level but to become intimate with and at one with it (Chopra 2000, 1).

God may be invisible, but He is the source of all miracles in the world. In 1929 Jung reminds us that "Only fools think that everything can be explained. The true substance of the world is inexplicable..." (Jung 1984, 172).

Jesus told us that we are also able to perform miracles, if we have faith. He said, "Truly, I tell you, if you have faith as small as a mustard seed, you can say to this mountain, 'Move from here to there,' and it will move. Nothing will be impossible for you" (Matthew, 17:20).

Spiritual Healing

The universal life force is an energy found within people as well as animals and plants. It is the only source of energy and matter that exists throughout the Universe. We are all interconnected within it.

Healing of many physical, emotional, and mental ailments takes place when a large amount of universal life force energy is infused into our bodies by grace or by divine intervention.

All spiritual healing is done by the universal life force and intelligence working through the healing intelligence of the body and through our faith. Faith is the strongest tool we possess in achieving healing and other miracles.

Healing takes place when high frequency energy is directed to the suffering part of an ill person. This high-frequency energy transmutes the heavy vibrations of the disease and illness, which block the flow of the vital life force through our body.

Every time we respond to someone in need and act out of love, empathy, and compassion towards him, we perform an act of power. The high frequency of love transmutes the lower vibrations of pain and fear, initiating the life force, which causes healing both in us and in others.

Ron Roth, a Roman Catholic Priest for more than twenty-five years and a spiritual healer who holds a B.A. in philosophy, an M.A. in theology, and a Ph.D. in religious studies writes in his book *The Healing Path of Prayer* that spiritual healing means unblocking the Spirit of God so that it can flow through our lives, changing and transforming us. It means learning to live in the Holy Spirit of wholeness and in the love of God in action by releasing the potential life of the divine that is always present within us (Roth 2010).

By thinking positively about our health, we can influence the energy level in our cells and we can alter their function. This proves miraculous in the case of cancer patients as well as other patients suffering from serious illnesses.

The levels of good chemicals, which make us feel well, increase with good thoughts and emotions, while the level of bad chemicals, which cause cardiovascular and gastrointestinal problems, decrease. Dr. Herbert Benson, the Harvard Medical School cardiologist, found out that patients who recite prayers, practice meditation, or repeat mantras can reduce stress, lower their metabolic rates, slow their heart rates and ease their pains (Benson, 1997).

So, for the healing process to take place, our consciousness needs to have the ability to connect with the Universal Healing Mind, which exists within our personal mind. To make that possible, we have to purify our energy. We have to increase our frequency by the energy of love, good intentions, faith, and compassion so that we can align ourselves with the Universal principles. By doing this, our energies match directly with the energy coming from the realm of infinite possibility and potential.

For spiritual healing to take place, the imbalance in our energy field must be restored and harmony must be established between our body, mind, and spirit.

We can achieve this harmony through higher levels of consciousness

- by becoming aware of major emotional issues and by eliminating them through forgiveness,

- by reviewing negative events and crises and finding the message and purpose they contain,
- by relieving problems caused by stress, anxiety, and depression,
- by activating our spiritual evolution by acts of love and service to others,
- by developing higher levels of conscious awareness and taking responsibility of our actions, and
- by being receptive to the healing powers.

The following is an extract of the healing meditation recited by Dr. P.L. Masters, the founder of the International Metaphysics Ministry. He recites,

> I turn away for few moments, breath by breath, from the world that surrounds me to enter into the world which is within me which contains the Infinite Mind of God. I synchronise my mind and my body's consciousness with the People who are not aware of the spiritual mysteries available in this universe and who do not have a strong faith cannot experience healing, as doubt blocks God's intervention.

An Example of Healing

A systematic, loving prayer by one or more people to improve the state of health of another person seems to release God's power and cause miracles to happen.

The power of community prayer sparked a healing miracle in Virginia in 2014 that doctors can't explain:

> The end of Grayson Kirby seemed inevitable when he was thrown from a demolition derby car at the Mid-Atlantic Power Festival in Ruckersville, VA, in June 2014. The accident left him in a coma. His lungs were crushed and nearly every other bone in his body was broken. His brain also suffered multiple strokes and hemorrhages and his kidneys were failing. If he did wake up, he would likely—to put it bluntly—be a vegetable. But his family refused to give up and turned to prayer. Thousands of people in the community and beyond kept Kirby in their thoughts and prayers and wore red shirts designed to show support for the injured man. In a final attempt to revive Kirby, doctors hooked him up to a machine typically used for transplant patients, not trauma patients. Whether it was due to a divine intervention or medical intervention (or both), it worked. Ten days after the accident, Kirby opened his eyes and mouthed the words, 'I love you,' to his father. The doctors couldn't believe it, and neither could Kirby. 'I'm humble, I'm grateful, just amazed' Kirby said. 'I know that God saved me. I know that prayer and believing saved me. (Schmidt 2015)

Forms Of Healing

Healing does not only mean returning to the previous state of health; it also means changing our whole attitude toward life.

When a tissue becomes injured, a change to its normal rate of vibration takes place, which causes the aching. The aim of the healing process is to restore the normal vibrational rate to the injured tissue, consequently alleviating pain and accelerating healing.

The most frequently applied and practiced form of healing involves the laying on of hands; it is almost an instinctive reaction to place one's hands on the area of the body where pain exists. So, the physical action of laying on of hands causes the energy level of the hands to come into contact with the energy field of that part of the body being healed. Healing energy gets transferred from one person to another in order to restore health.

Spiritual healing can be instantaneous and it can take place from a long distance too.

If you are in a low state of consciousness, when you feel low energy, or when you are stressed and irritable, avoid practicing healing as your negative energy could be transferred to the other person. Raise your consciousness first. The easiest and fastest way to accomplish higher states of consciousness is to abandon your personal state of consciousness and to reach God consciousness by meditating.

Disease

Disease should be seen as a message from the body in the form of a physical symptom when an imbalance exists between our body, mind, and spirit and when we live a life deprived of love, compassion, or any other spiritual value. It is a notification to change our whole attitude in life, in order to enable the healing process to take place.

Medical doctors might have diagnosed many people with a serious disease, sometimes in their lives. Some of these people have managed to regain their health again, either due to the help of the medical fraternity or because of their involvement with one of the numerous ways and practices of spiritual healing.

Thoughts of anger, fear, and anxiety produce changes in the chemistry of the brain, which cause detrimental effects in the physiology of our body and initiate the onset of disease.

Try to do more unselfish acts of kindness, entertain more joyful and fulfilling thoughts, and spread unconditional love to every part of the creation, in order to increase the frequency of your vibrations. Start the healing process in your inner and outer selves by becoming channels of divine energy from the higher source.

A Miraculous Healing at Lourdes.

Lourdes is a small town located in the Hautes-Pyrénées region of France, famous for the Marian apparitions that are said to have occurred there in 1858. The town is named after the grotto of Massabielle, where the Virgin Mary is said to have appeared to a young girl named Bernadette Soubirous.

Lourdes has become a major Catholic pilgrimage site, with millions of visitors each year coming to pray, attend mass, and seek healing at the waters of the spring that flows from the grotto. The town is also home to the Sanctuary of Our Lady of Lourdes, a complex of churches and chapels built around the grotto, as well as several hospitals and other facilities that cater to the needs of the many pilgrims who come to Lourdes (https://en.wikipedia.org/wiki/Lourdes).

The cure of Vittorio Micheli at Lourdes is another example of the miraculous cure of a sarcoma of the pelvis:

In April 1962, Vittorio Micheli, a soldier in the Italian Army, developed rapidly increasing pain in his left buttock region. X-rays of the left hip showed osteolysis involving the ilium and the roof of the acetabulum. A biopsy of the gluteal muscle showed cells of a sarcomatous character. He was not deemed to be a candidate for medical intervention, so neither radiotherapy nor chemotherapy was offered to him. In May 1963, racked with pain and unable to walk, he made a pilgrimage to Lourdes, following which he was cured of his sarcoma. The International Medical Committee of Lourdes reviewed his case in 1969 and in 1971. There was unanimous agreement that this was a medically inexplicable cure. (Neilan B, Scientific contributions, Article Aug 2013)

CHAPTER NINE

"How you vibrate is what the universe
echoes back to you in every moment."

Panache

VIBRATIONS

Everything in nature is made up of vibrations of energy. All objects in our world are energy fields that vibrate at different frequencies. Our bodies are electromagnetic fields that vibrate at about 7.5 Hz when we are standing and at about 4 to 6 Hz when we are sitting down. Our minds are also electromagnetic fields. These two fields do interact with each other. This interaction makes them interconnected and interdependent on each other. This vibrating motion, together with the different patterns of vibration, produces waves.

We all have our own vibrating system. It is the life force energy without which we cannot live. We humans in the material form manifest only specific energy frequencies that we can apprehend by our senses. Our human senses are only able to perceive what vibrates within certain ranges of frequency within this physical realm.

The food we eat, the drinks we consume, the thoughts we make, the emotions we feel, and the different frequencies of energy we receive from the people around us automatically affect this vibrating system. According to the law of cause and effect in our Universe all our actions, words, deeds, and thoughts create good, bad, or neutral types of vibrations, which influence our whole beings.

Frequencies

Our body is influenced by the frequency of the vibrations of different specific emotional states. Frequencies of over 700 Hz, correspond to the state of enlightenment and super-consciousness. Enlightenment, which means to be embodied with spiritual light and be spiritually awakened, has the highest frequency of 700+ Hz and the greatest expansion of energy. Examples of those frequencies are the sounds of meditation, spiritual and healing pieces of music.

Frequencies of 432 Hz and higher make us relaxed and calm and have healing properties in the body. When we play or listen to music of 432 Hz, we feel happier and more content, and when we reach the vibrational frequency of 540 Hz, we feel more joyous and blissful. Examples of this type of music are the classical pieces.

Certain frequencies can negatively change our mood, our feelings, and even our health. Low frequencies of under 20 Hz, like the ones we find in extreme bass sound, trigger the release of stress hormones causing fear and anxiety in us. The same happens if we are exposed to background noise in urban environments like air-conditioning, ventilation, compressors, traffic, etc. They affect negatively our physiological and psychological states of being.

Rates of Vibrations

The frequency rates at which we vibrate define the different dimensions in which we can exist. Dimensions are different planes of existence with their own rates of vibrations, which are in tune with the frequency of that dimension.

The consciousness in the first dimension, in the physical form with the DNA as its foundation, is molecular consisting of protons, electrons, nuclei, atoms, minerals, water, and genetic codes.

Raising our vibrations enables us to receive direct guidance and information from our higher self. It exposes us to higher levels of consciousness, resulting in elevated intuition, increased telepathy, clairvoyance, healing, and inner peace, joy, and harmony.

The state of our health and well-being in general is in direct proportion to the amount of universal or spiritual energy we accept. It also depends on how freely the energy flows through us and how well we transmit it. The more life force energy we get through our breathing and through our nourishment, and the more we transmit it to other people and to nature around us, the healthier and more content we become.

According to the spiritual law of frequency and vibration, when we live our lives with honesty, love, compassion, goodness, faith, generosity, and joy we automatically neutralize the low frequency emissions of others around us and we transmute them to a high frequency vibration. All negative thoughts and feelings of anger, jealousy, violence, guilt, and wickedness produce heavy, low frequency vibrations.

In order to attract positive experiences, positive coincidences and healthy relationships, we need to live and operate at a high vibrational frequency energy. We need to realize at all times that our thoughts are extremely powerful.

Hold a positive viewpoint at every situation, try to replace any dark negative energy in your mind by the higher white light of God's presence, neutralize any problem, and you will change the way this Universe manifests through and around you.

Based on the findings of the following experiment in which 2,000 people participated in Tokyo. The Japanese researcher and healer, Dr. Masaru Emoto, conducted experiments on water molecules. He asked the candidates to infuse different types of thoughts into bottles of water. He then froze the bottles and he examined the water crystals under a microscope. He consequently discovered that the water crystals infused with thoughts of higher vibrations like positive thoughts of love or joy or happiness formed different patterns which were orderly and beautiful in contrast with the crystals which were infused with negative thoughts of hate, anger, and envy, which seemed to be chaotic(https:// thewellnessenterprise.com/emoto/).

Keeping in mind that 75% of the human body is water, it is easy to understand that our thoughts do influence our bodily health.

Wave Patterns

Wave patterns are patterns of vibrations, which may or may not be picked up by our five senses.

Wavelength is the distance between repeating crests or troughs of a wave pattern. This pattern determines their frequency. Frequency refers to the measurement of the number of times that a repeated event occurs per unit of time, such as per second. The frequency of a wave is the number of cycles that pass a given point of observation per second. The unit of measurement is the hertz.

If we drop two stones into a pond, concentric circles or waves radiate and move across the pond. Where the crests of those waves meet, they make a wave that is twice as high, which is called an interference pattern; if a wave meets a trough, the two will cancel each other out to form a flat patch; if two troughs meet, they will make a deeper trough. If two identical light waves with the same wavelength overlap with each other, we get a much brighter light. This is called constructive interference.

We perceive the physical world through our five senses, because objects vibrate and send out waves of light, sound, and smell through the air. Where there is no light, we can only perceive sound, an example of which is the ultrasonic wave. We do receive thought vibrations in our various emotional, mental, and spiritual states of consciousness.

The Dutch physicist, astronomer and mathematician, Christian Huygens, in 1656 after having performed a series of experiments with swinging pendulum, found out that pendula of similar lengths swinging randomly do begin to swing in unison after a period of time. He named this phenomenon "the principle of entrainment". According to the principle of entrainment, weaker pulsations come under the influence of stronger ones.

The British naturopath Dr. Peter Guy Manners used the principle of entrainment in the treatment of a variety of physiological conditions based on the hypothesis that every bodily organ has a certain size, shape, and density; therefore, it vibrates within its own specific range of frequencies.

Dr. Manners recorded the resonant frequencies of healthy tissues and organs. He devised a way to project these vibrations via sound waves directly into distressed areas, which were not resonating at their proper, healthy frequencies. Through a process called sympathetic resonance, he guided tissues back to their optimal frequency patterns, while releasing the tension they had been storing.

PART FIVE

The Psychic Aspect

"The key to growth is the introduction of higher dimensions of consciousness into our awareness."

Laozi

CHAPTER TEN

"The mystery of sound is mysticism;
The harmony of life is religion."
Hazrat Inayat Khan

RELIGION

Religion is the world's largest, most functional, and most organized social structure. It deals with the human need for spirituality and its yearning for immortality.

In all civilizations the prevailing religion of the era has been mirrored in art, literature, and philosophy. All religions in this world have helped humanity tremendously. They helped people to find meaning in life either through ritualistic practices, prayers, or through supernatural narratives.

When religions are manipulated by politics they can become a deadly threat to humanity, defeating their actual spiritual function of promoting spirituality and spreading love, goodness, and peace.

The Goal of Religion?

People are very confused about the goal and the purpose of religion and of spirituality. Some think that the purpose of all religions is to forge people's conscience. Others consider religion to be the path to personal happiness, to personal satisfaction, and to their connection with the Universal Mind.

History suggests that the concept of a superior entity or God has always existed in people and that the same intrinsic need for a deity continues to exist today.

The task of different religions in the world is

- to lead their followers to God consciousness, which is the ultimate spiritual attainment,
- to give them the necessary knowledge of how to achieve it and
- to instruct them with the rules and regulations of their religious organization.

Karen Armstrong, a British author of Irish Catholic descent, writes in her seminal book *A History of God* that because human beings cannot endure emptiness, they fill their vacuum by creating a new focus in their lives, in order to find meaning. By doing so, a new spirituality is emerging, the purpose of which is to be practiced in our daily lives, beyond church walls. She says that the difference between the dogmas of traditional religion and spiritual living is worth examining by all of us (Armstrong 1994).

Many of us were raised within a certain faith, with its traditions and beliefs. It is a fact that our affiliation with our religion has served us as our foundation, our security, and our pillar of hope and strength in times of challenge or doubt. So, we never questioned those beliefs and traditions, which over the years have gradually changed, in order to adapt to the needs of various cultures.

Christianity today is a multilanguage and multicultural religion with many debates over ethics and practices. Some Christians may reject a certain practice, while others gladly accept them. The Jesuits permitted the Chinese converts to honor their ancestors, while the Dominicans and Franciscans considered it to be a form of idolatry. Colonial missionaries in Africa were opposed to polygamy. In today's world, the questions of homosexuality and abortion continue to fuel debates among the Christian churches.

CHAPTER ELEVEN

"Do unto others as you would have them do unto you."
Luke 6:31

CHRISTIANITY

Christianity is one of the world's biggest religions, with about 2.5 billion followers worldwide. It is a monotheistic religion based on the teachings and the examples of Jesus Christ who lived in the Holy Land 2,000 years ago. The life and teachings of Jesus are presented in the canonical Gospels, in the Apocrypha, and in the other New Testament writings.

Christianity is a religion of personal insight and spiritual growth. It teaches that Jesus, the Messiah is the incarnated son of God and the saviour of humanity. He is one with God and the Holy Spirit.

Christianity is based on truth, the true word, and the true living. It is based on the principles of forgiveness, compassion, service, and love and on the core values of justice, mercy, and kindness, which take precedence over everything else. It aims to lead the devotees to their esoteric planes of existence and to their full realization of the Christ Mind and of the Christ Consciousness. The followers of the Christian faith are known as Christians.

Christian faith opens up a different way to look at the world. It is like a good pair of glasses. Looking through the corrective lenses of Christian teachings, we are able to clear our vision and see the beauty of God's creative order.

We are not Christians because of our occasional attendance of a church service, regular prayer, or Bible reading. We are Christians because Christianity offers us a comprehensive way to think about right and wrong and to interpret life's ordinary, as well as extraordinary events accordingly.

The Golden Rule of Christianity is expressed in the following words of Jesus: If you love those who love you, what credit is that to you? Even sinners love those who love them. And if you do good to those who are good to you, what credit is that to you? Even sinners do that. And if you lend to those from whom you expect repayment, what credit is that to you? Even sinners lend to sinners, expecting to be repaid in full. But love your enemies, do good to them, and lend to them without expecting to get anything back. Then your reward will be great, and you will be sons of the Most High, because He is kind to the ungrateful and wicked (Luke 6:31-35).

Esoteric Christianity

Esoteric ideas occupy a predominant place in the four Gospels of the New Testament and in the John of Patmos

Revelation. All esotericism begins with the belief that something higher exists that lies beyond what our five senses can perceive. There is a higher reality, which we can only contact spiritually.

To be able to achieve that, we should have a clear awareness of who we really are without being bounded and defined by time and space. That is exactly what Jesus meant, according to mystics, when he mentioned "being in the World but not of the World" (Romans, 12:2). He meant being in higher states of consciousness, while still in the physical form.

The purpose of esoteric Christianity is to take us beyond the level of the individual ego. It is to awaken the dormant light of our divinity, which lies inside our minds. It is to help us develop another higher state of awareness in order to free ourselves from the tyranny of the ego and from the chaotic state of the mind.

We must remember that we are not human beings who are searching for Spirit, but we are Spirits trying to live in the human form so that the oneness of God can be reflected by us in all our expressions of life.

Realize that there should be no separation between body, mind, soul, and spirit. They should all be integrated, because the integration of all these three parts in us gives us the good health and the strength to sail through this life in peace.

Christian Morality

Morality is a system of standards and types of behaviour.

Our sense of morality plays a very important role in our everyday decisions. It shapes up our behaviour as we go through our days and conduct our business. Eventually, this sense of morality changes with time or as a result of some traumatic events like wars or catastrophes.

Different people do normally talk about "morality" in a relative term rather than in an absolute term. This means that morality is culturally defined. People of different cultures have different moral standards relative to their legal and religious belief system. In most systems, morality is normally based on virtue and on what is considered to be virtuous. The good and virtuous eventually get compensated by salvation, and the non-virtuous gets punished by excommunication and suffering.

Christian morality implies living and acting as close as possible to standards laid down by Jesus. It evokes in us a sense of moral responsibility, from which the voice of our conscience originates and our moral profile gets formed.

There are many standards of morality in this world. Just to mention few, there is the Christian morality, the Jewish morality, the morality of the different cultures in different geographic regions, or the morality of the Ancient Greeks. In other words, morality seems to be a code of conduct that we, as members of a certain society, ethnic group, tribe or religion, adopt for a certain period of time.

In Judaism, virtue and virtuous living means obedience to the Mosaic Law and living according to the ten commandments. There is no half way measure; one is either obedient or not, virtuous or not, good or bad, evil or holy.

Some Christians too, in a very simplistic and most Judaic way, most often feel that if they have not committed one of the major transgressions prescribed in the Ten Commandments and if they have fasted, they are worthy of receiving Holy Communion as a reward for their virtuous behaviour. Yet, we read in the divine liturgy that no one is worthy of the Holy Communion, in spite of any virtuous living or fasting and praying preparation. Only by the Grace of God we become able to participate in the body of Christ and have a chance of transforming our human nature into the likeness of God.

On the subject of Jewish fasting or following certain dietary restrictions, Jesus said to his disciples, "Don't you see that nothing that enters a man from the outside can make him unclean? For it doesn't go into his heart but into his stomach, and then out of his body". He went on to say, "What comes out of a man is what makes him unclean. For from within, out of men's hearts, come evil thoughts, sexual immorality, theft, murder, adultery, greed, malice, deceit, envy, slander, arrogance and folly. All these evils come from inside and make a man unclean" (Mark 7: 14-23).

Christian morality is based only in truth. Jesus said, "I am the way, the truth and the life" (John, 14:6). Christian morality has to do with the person's real self, his actual identity, and not the roles he plays in society and the masks he wears in order to be accepted and praised by his fellow human beings.

The Christian doctrine is not based upon the dualistic system of right and wrong or on virtues, but rather on being truthful with oneself and inside one's heart and mind. It is not what one does that is important but who one is. It is not just conforming to the law but believing in it. It is not "what God wants us to do", which relates to obedience, but rather "what would Jesus do"? that should determine our actions as an act of faithful imitation.

We often have to compromise our morality though at a personal level either to avoid trouble or for personal justifications or for personal gains. Doing something correctly is an external, pride-producing, and ego-inflating practice leading consequently to feelings of superiority and self-righteousness. This is the exact opposite of what any Christian should try to achieve. Jesus, in the parable of the "Pharisee and the tax collector", spoke about some people who are so confident of their own righteousness and so very proud of themselves for keeping the Mosaic Law and helping the poor that they look down upon everyone else (Luke 18: 10-14).

The purpose of Christian morality is not to improve one's outward behaviour only. It is an inner action of transforming one's mind and reason, in order to achieve a higher consciousness of awareness of the divine truth and to live accordingly.

Truth, love and goodness, being attributes of the soul, are the only important components in a Christian's life. Love is the creative energy of this Universe. God is love, both in essence and energy. The matching relationship between this divine love and the human love is what results in real and true morality and what any Christian should strive for.

Goodness is produced when our actions are derived from our elevated awareness and they match the divine truth and the divine will. The good in Christianity is identified with God. Jesus asked, "Why do you ask me about what is good? None is good except God" (Matthew, 19:16).

Accordingly, anything that matches the divine Good is good, it is moral and it is ethical. In practical terms, it is about more compassion, less judgment, more love, less hate, more forgiveness, and less punishment.

A Saint and a Scorpion

An example of goodness is the story about the saint and a scorpion:

> One day a saint went to a river to bathe. There he noticed a scorpion struggling in the water near him. Scorpions cannot swim, and the saint knew that if he did not save the scorpion, it would drown.
>
> Therefore, the saint carefully picked up the struggling scorpion, trying to rescue it out from the water. But as he was just about to set it on land, the scorpion stung his finger. The sharp pain from the sting made the saint instinctively fling his hand, and the scorpion went flying back into the water. As soon as the saint gained his

composure from the pain, he attempted to rescue the troubled creature again. But, as earlier, the scorpion stung him again before he could safely keep it on the land. So, the affair repeated several times as the saint continued his attempt to save the scorpion while the creature attacked its savior every time. The saint's disciples watched the event for a while and were worried for the saint, who was now staggering from the pain. The disciple requested the saint to leave the vicious creature on its own. The saint ignored the request from his disciples and continued his attempt to save the scorpion until he finally succeeded. The disciples carried the reeling saint to his hut, treated him for his wounds and waited for the saint to get well. After the saint regained consciousness, one of the disciples asked him why the saint let the scorpion attack him several times and continued to help it. The saint replied, "My dear child, the scorpion did not sting me out of malice or evil intent. Just as it is the water's nature to make things wet and fire's nature to burn, it is in the scorpion's nature to sting. The ignorant creature kept stinging me because its comprehension was not significant enough to realize that I was trying to help him. But just as it is the scorpion's nature to sting, so it is my nature to save. Just as he did not leave his nature, why should I leave my nature? I must help any soul in need. I should not let the stings from a scorpion rob me from performing my duty as a savior". (Swami Chidananda 2011)

Sin in Christianity

Sin is an immoral act which transgresses the divine law, according to the Judaic religions of Judaism, Christianity, and Islam. Committing a sin is considered to be associated with rules that, when broken, have punishment as a consequence.

This is not the actual meaning of the word "sin". The ancient Greek word for sin is "hamartia" which means, "to miss the mark" (Wikipedia 2021). Like in archery or in darts, we are trying to hit the centre, the bullseye, and anytime we deviate even an inch from the centre we miss the mark, therefore we sin.

For us Christians, the goal of Christian life is to be Christ-like. It is about keeping Christ in our sight and keeping Him at the centre of our consciousness. Any type of distraction and any deviation from that, anything we do that takes us away from the love of God, away from the experience of God, away from the spiritual life, is technically missing the mark; it is moving away from our life source; therefore, it is a sin.

The suppression of natural impulses does not raise the consciousness of the spiritual self. Our existence here upon the Earth is for the purpose of learning through experience. One may indulge freely in those things, which are constructive and good and injurious to none.

In today's world, the seven deadly sins, which should be avoided by any devotee, are considered to be:

- sloth,
- gluttony,
- lust,
- greed,
- pride,
- envy,
- wrath.

Christian Churches

Human societies are structured according to certain systems of thought and action that we call "principles". Our principles influence our daily behaviour, and they constitute our culture.

Christianity began as a Jewish sect in the mid-first century. It started in the region of modern Israel and Palestine, and it quickly spread to Syria, Mesopotamia, Asia Minor, and Egypt.

Jesus, with his teachings and his new way of thinking, challenged all those very human structures that existed in his time. He proclaimed a new relationship with God. He taught new ideas and new principles of truth to people who had an old way of life and an old religion which were not conducive to God's revelation. He knew that the new way of life that he was promoting was drastically different than what the others were teaching. People had become too much set in their ways and their laws. They had closed their minds to new ideas about God and how He reveals Himself to his people.

During the Middle Ages, most of Europe was Christianized. Through colonization and hence through missionary work, Christianity spread to the Americas, Australia, sub-Saharan Africa, and the rest of the World. Christian missionaries following Jesus' commands to love and serve others, established hospitals, churches, schools, charities, orphanages, homeless shelters, and universities in the areas in which they spread Christianity.

When the Church became an organization rather than a movement for spiritual development and higher conscious-ness, the early Christian Church consciously or uncon-sciously translated the metaphysical principles of Jesus into dogmatic religious principles. Some of Jesus' teachings lost their meaning completely, as for many Christians the tradi-tions, the rituals, the laws, and regulations of the structure of the Church became primary and prevalent and the teachings of the Gospel secondary.

The three largest denominations in the world of Christianity are the original Orthodox Church, the Roman Catholic Church and the various denominations of Protestantism.

"The Eastern Orthodox Church is the second-largest Christian Church, with approximately 220 million baptised members. It operates as a communion of autocephalous churches governed by its bishops" (Wikipedia, 2019).

'The Catholic Church, also known as the Roman Catholic Church, is the largest Christian Church and the largest religious denomination, with approximately 1.3 billion baptised Catholics worldwide as of 2019" (Wikipedia, 2019). It is also governed by its bishops, archbishops, and the Pope of Rome.

Protestantism is a form of Christianity that originated with the sixteenth -century reformation. It started as a movement against what its followers perceived to be errors in the Catholic Church (Wikipedia, 2021).

Unfortunately, heads of the Christian Churches differ in their interpretations of the Christian Bible, and many Christians have the tendency to substitute the word "Jesus Christ" for the organization "Church" that promotes and teaches the word of God. Some Christians also tend to forget that only the truth of the teachings of Jesus can radically change human lives, irrespective of the denomination they get exposed to.

Have we perhaps confused the truth of God's word, which is constantly being revealed to us, with the traditions and regulations of the structure that holds it? Have our cultural rituals prevailed over our devotion? Do we perhaps continue our old ways of practicing without thinking because change requires effort and it is not as comfortable, easy, and predictable? Have our own spiritual lives lost their elasticity to accommodate the Spirit of God? Do we stick to the old structures and principles automatically without considering a new way of thinking and acting based on the teachings of Jesus, in order to receive spiritual enlightenment?

CHAPTER TWELVE

"One of the greatest regrets in life is being what others
would want you to be, rather than being yourself."
Shannon L. Alder

REAL OR HIGHER SELF

Our real or higher self is our divine part, which is perfect. It
exists within each one of us, waiting to be discovered. The
biggest achievement in the spiritual path is to recognize
the existence of our higher self, or soul. It is to hear that
inner voice and to accept the notion that something higher
transcends everything else in this world. Knowing our soul's
purpose is the most important key to a meaningful, enthusiastic, highly motivated, and happy life.

Our real self is pure and close to the eternal, all loving
presence of God. It is real because it is part of God who
is real and not illusionary like our false sense of identity.
It is part of a higher dimension of profound stillness, of
silence, and of space. It is connected to the absolute truth,

and as such, it lives in the "now". It experiences the "now" without any thinking but just by getting wisdom and receiving inspirations.

Although, our real self exists without the use of our material senses, it uses our brains to function, our eyes to see, our ears to hear, as well as all our other senses, in order to survive in this material world. Our real selves experience no anger, no hate, no fear, and no prejudices, but pure joy, bliss, love, and peace. It is the state of a newborn or very young baby. This is the state we were in before we became who we think we are. That is the reason that Jesus said, "Truly, I tell you, unless you change and become like little children, you will never enter the Kingdom of Heaven" (Matthew 18:3).

People who have discovered their soul's purpose for this lifetime have discovered that they have a divine destiny, and they have turned their lives over to a high force. They have taken time to tune into the higher consciousness within themselves and surrender themselves to the divine.

When we realize the existence of our pure self and we separate our brain activity of thoughts and emotions from our consciousness, our life changes totally. Our relationships with other people improve; we realize that there is no bad person and no one is wrong. We forgive others and ourselves as God always forgives our trespasses, hears our prayers, and he is there for us. Albert Einstein stated, "Weak people get revenge, strong people forgive, and intelligent people ignore" (Einstein 2012).

Mystics have frequently said that the path to union with God or to God's realization comes from within each individual, meaning that the divine and the soul are one and the same. Our ability to observe our true selves as a separate presence in our body and to realize that our true self is part of the Divine Intelligence and Love causes the energy field that surrounds us to vibrate at a higher frequency. As a result, our rate of vibrations increases, our conscious awareness expands, and our personal sensitivity to the energies around us improve. We notice the positive changes in our feelings and emotions. Our lives are filled with physical and mental healing, with creativity, with optimism, with hope and with success in our everyday life.

Most people try to distract their thoughts as if they want to cease being aware of life. They are not brave enough to face reality. This may cause a great void of emptiness within people that can lead to alcohol, drugs, gambling, or neurotic relationships. A life without knowing one's soul's purpose is a life without meaning, without hope, inspiration or happiness.

Immortality of the Higher Self

At the time of death, the higher self or soul is released from the human body in which it was contained and it rejoins the Universal Energy in order to become part of the whole again. Its state of being depends on the imprint of its own experiences of happiness and suffering, which the real self, or soul is carrying at the time of death.

One of the foundations of the Christian faith is the belief in the immortality of the soul and in life after the death of the body. Christians regard the soul as the immortal essence of a human being and they refer to it in a moral rather than in a philosophical way. They believe that when a person dies his soul, which has been affected by his way of life and by the good or evil deeds he has committed, gets judged by God and consequently gets rewarded or punished.

If the soul is part of the undifferentiated energy from which all matter emerges mysteriously when life starts, then when death occurs, that soul energy becomes part of that whole again. Death then is not a state of "nothingness" but of "every thingness" and "hell" or "paradise" do not exist as actual places but just as states of consciousness.

Aristotle defined the soul as the core essence of a being, as a "form of a natural body that has life potentially" (Aristotle, Reeve C., II 1 412a,19-21). He argued against it having a separate existence and being immortal. He considered the intellect to be eternal, to be part of the soul and separable from the body. He said, "The highest level of the soul is occupied by mind or reason, the locus of thought and under-standing" (Aristotle, 2021).

Plato, drawing on the words of his teacher Socrates, considered the soul as the incorporeal, eternal essence of a person, which occupies our form and is responsible for our behaviour. He further believed that when the carnal bodies die, the soul, which comprises the mind, the emotion, and the desires, gets trapped into a continuous cycle of rebirths into subsequent bodies. Each of these three parts of the soul plays an important role in a balanced and peaceful soul.

I believe that our higher self already exists at a higher plane. It always existed there, since our physical birth and even before. It is another dimensional energy body that is part of one of the other dimensions or states of existence that constitute our beingness.

A Childhood Story

When I was seven years old, I met a man named Chris who was on a journey to discover the meaning of life. He had spent many years studying philosophy and religion, trying to find the answers to the mysteries of this Universe. One day, while meditating in the mountains, he had a revelation. He realized that the true essence of a person was their higher self, the immortal part of themselves that existed beyond the physical body.

Chris became convinced that the higher self was the key to immortality, and he dedicated his life to exploring this concept further. He traveled to remote monasteries in the world and studied with spiritual masters, learning all he could about the higher self and how to tap into its power.

As he dove deeper into his studies, Chris began to experience strange and miraculous events. He discovered that he had the ability to communicate with his higher self at will and that this connection gave him access to knowledge and wisdom far beyond what he could have ever imagined.

Through his meditations and spiritual practices, Chris was able to tap into the full potential of his higher self, and he began to live a life of great purpose and meaning. He was no longer bound by the limitations of his physical body, and he experienced a sense of freedom and joy that he had never known before.

He realized that the higher self was truly immortal and that it would continue to exist long after his physical body had passed away. He understood that it was the higher self that was the true essence of a person and that it was the key to achieving true happiness and fulfillment in life.

So, Chris spent the rest of his days spreading this message, his wisdom, and insights to me and to anyone who would listen and who wanted to learn.

He became a beacon of light, guiding myself and others on our own journey towards enlightenment, to the eternal knowledge of the higher self.

CHAPTER THIRTEEN

"A human being is a part of the whole called by us universe, a part limited in time and space. He experiences himself, his thoughts and feeling as something separated from the rest, a kind of optical delusion of his consciousness."

Albert Einstein

METAPHYSICS

Metaphysics is the science that focuses on and researches what lies beyond the physical existence. It considers the physical world to be the manifestation of an invisible force of a metaphysical nature.

Metaphysics is based on the idea that the world we perceive through our five senses is not the real world but an illusion of our senses, as we see everything through our own personal brain filters, which prevent us from seeing the actual reality.

All metaphysical teachings teach one basic truth, which says that here is but one mind in the Universe and that all individual minds are individualized expressions of that one mind and inseparable parts of it.

Benefits of the Study of Metaphysics

By gaining knowledge of Metaphysics,

- we can develop our spiritual nature to such an extent that we can achieve a better understanding of life,
- we can experience a direct connection with the divine,
- we can avoid the pain and disappointments which are encountered daily in this material, sensory world,
- we can shape our own destiny by controlling our emotional and thought processes.

CHAPTER FOURTEEN

"Consciousness cannot be accounted for in physical
terms. For consciousness is absolutely fundamental. It
cannot be accounted for in terms of anything else."
Erwin Schrödinger

CONSCIOUSNESS

Consciousness can be defined as the sum total of a person's
conscious awareness. It includes one's sense of spirit, soul and
body. It includes the accumulation of all his ideas, thoughts,
emotions, sensations, and knowledge.

Human consciousness creates its own reality based on
one's beliefs, attitudes, fears, hopes, and memories. The words
"wakefulness" and "consciousness" are often used as the same
meaning in medicine. When medicine uses the term "loss
of consciousness", in reality it means "loss of wakefulness"
during which certain bodily functions have been shut down
for the cessation of pain.

Based on the full-time research that has been conducted since 1959 by Dr. P. L. Masters and other researchers into the exploration of consciousness, we are responsible of how we see the events in our life, how we interpret them and how we appreciate them. These findings were based on the synthesis of their research results with science, psychology, and mystical teachings.

God has given us the ability to access our guiding consciousness, which is capable of controlling our mind. Only humans on this planet have the neurological capability to access the dimension of consciousness, which is beyond the physical boundaries. No other creature can access it, even though they have consciousness because they have life. Therefore, our body has the ability to access our mind, our mind to access our consciousness and our consciousness to access God.

Human Consciousness

The human consciousness, which contains the total of all the physical, emotional, mental and spiritual aspects of every human being manifests different vibrating energies of different frequencies.

Our five senses help us survive in this physical dimension by giving us information about the physical world and the physical dimension that surrounds us and in which we live. Our belief system, which depends solely on our five senses, our intellect, and our memory, molds and affects our reality.

Our five senses can only perceive a certain type of frequency and not any frequency of the higher dimensions, which are the spiritual and the divine dimensions. In order to be aware of the higher dimensions, we need to transcend this reality by developing an advanced spiritual awareness through which we can rise to a higher level of consciousness.

When we replace our personal ego with the unlimited sense of God's presence within us, we reach the higher level of consciousness as God takes over the conscious level of our mind. We then feel free from all the ideas and all the limitations in our mind, as well as from all our past memories and experiences.

Ego Consciousness

Human ego consciousness is a continuum. On the one extreme side humans identify with their material selves, and on the other extreme, they identify with their higher self.

The spiritual goal of most spiritual teachings is the minimization of the ego and the experiencing of the true nature of the human being, through self-knowledge.

Our personal growth in consciousness is a struggle between two elements of our own mind: our higher self, which desires to achieve God Consciousness, and our lower, ego- dominated self, which wants to continue to identify with this illusionary world. We are trapped in this duality. We need to transcend the duality in order to have the mystical experience that there is something beyond the physical realm.

What obstructs our inner development is our ego. Our ego belongs to the social level of consciousness, or the lowest dimension of existence. Our thoughts, beliefs, convictions, and emotions greatly influence our actual behaviour, and they become our only reality. They are most often rooted in our life's past events, experiences, and conditionings.

Our conditionings and upbringing are responsible for craving for food, wealth, status, position, power, sex, intimacy, or attention from others. Our desires are endless and can never be totally satisfied. Einstein said, "The true measure of a human being is determined primarily by the measure and sense in which he has attained liberation from the self" (Einstein, 2017).

Our ego-based thinking is the main source of different stresses in our lives as it makes us live in a continuous state of fear and insecurity, which comprises amongst others the fear of change, the fear of criticism, the fear of rejection, the fear of loss, and the fear of death. It continuously filters reality through language, through judging and labelling, causing us endless suffering, craving and aversion. The illusionary ego clings to power as a form of protection and it thrives on recognition and acceptance. It can only experience love as a need and possessiveness and it only gives in order to receive.

As long as our thinking remains the same, as long as we use self-justification and negativity, we remain the slaves of our egos. If we identify with the illusionary self, we live in darkness; if we identify with our personality and the role we play in society, we live with the illusion of the self, which is conditioned by the rules and regulations of society.

We must realize though, that we are not our egos, we are not our thoughts, and we are not our emotions. We are our pure real selves, which is part of God, our Creator, and which manifest throughout our bodies and our brains in the physical life.

We have a natural tendency to want to blame something outside ourselves for the state of the world. We sometimes blame another person, another country, or another religion. We should realize that we are the only responsible beings because we are mainly governed by many little conditionings and programs from the past. Only if we stop judging our thoughts as good or bad, if we drop all our existing labels, if we completely stop identifying with our ego identity, it is possible to see things as they are.

We need to allow the Infinite Light to remove our personal ego together and all the mental debris that we have collected through the years so that God's presence can reach us and create for us whatever we really need. We have to see another dimension to our life and a new way of perceiving the world.

Every step we take in the continuum towards the realization of the real self, less our suffering will become in this life. Less suffering does not mean that life is free of pain. It means that we realize that there is something more than the material world and self-interest, and we show less resistance to it as our perspective on life changes. We realize that stress is not caused by external factors, but by the combination of external factors in conjunction with the interpretation of our conditioned brain and the voice of our own thoughts.

Two thousand four hundred years ago, Plato wrote in his book *The Republic* about the people who were chained in a cave all their lives, facing a blank wall and seeing only shadows on it. The shadows were the only known reality to these people. Even when they heard that there was something more, they were afraid to leave what was familiar. Humanity is still trying to get out of "Plato's Cave." To be realistic, we are more attached to illusions now than we ever have been (Plato, Bloom 2016).

The shadows are analogous to our thoughts. The world of our thoughts is the only world we know. It is frightening for us to stop relying on our thoughts, to start looking for who we really are, and to trust the Light. While we have been used to living in darkness, we must slowly get used to living in the light.

Rene Descartes, the famous western philosopher, is known for the saying, "I think therefore I am" (Levene, 2010), equating the fundamental human being with thinking. This shows us the extent of our identification with our thinking or the shadows on the cave wall.

We can free ourselves of our conditioned mind from past concepts by simply observing it in action and being fully aware of it. Thus, we can actually become free; we can avoid unnecessary pain and great suffering.

As long as our thinking remains the same, as long as we use self-justification and negativity, we remain the slaves of our egos and our past conditioning.

We need to let go of the life that is inherited from the past to achieve the life that will come through the inner world. *William Shakespeare,* the famous English playwright, poet, and actor of the sixteenth century, referring to the illusionary lives we live, mentions in his comedy "As you like it," that "All the world is a stage and all men and women are players" (Murray 1996, p 4).

We can be awakened from the play of life. We can become aware of our real selves; we can stop identifying with our characters, believing that we are the role we are playing, and give up wearing our mask and playing our social role.

When the ego is submissive to the inner real self then the soul is in harmony with itself, with the world, and with God.

Expanded Consciousness

Our expanded consciousness gives us access to enlighten-ment and to higher conscious awareness. It elevates us to the contact point between the divine mind and the human thought. It gives us access to our inner wisdom and to intu-ition for the solution of any problem that our rational mind cannot cope with.

Most of us think that we are free, conscious and awake. If we believe that, it will be very difficult to attain what we believe that we already have. Before we are awakened to higher levels of conscious awareness, we have to accept and realize that we are asleep and that we live a repetitive, automatic robotic-like life, avoiding pain and seeking pleasure. We should stop thinking that our ideas and our beliefs are real and not simply the creations of our minds.

When we become aware of our robot-like nature, we start the process of becoming more awake and start to recognise the problem. Once we recognize the problem, it is easier to stop the pathological thinking of identifying with the limited self, which enslaves our divine essence.

All people carry a greater power within themselves, a power that they are not aware of. It is a deeper Intelligence that God has given to each person, a perfect guiding Intelligence within everyone. It is called higher conscious awareness, and it comes with enlightenment. It is the Mind of God within everyone, which exists beyond one's intellect and beyond one's understanding. It is not governed by fear of loss and deprivation, by grievances and distrust. It is not conditioned by our culture, parents, or society. It is not influenced by any feeling or emotion. It is pure and powerful giving us protection and guidance. It is part of the greater reality that is not limited by space and time.

We can actively choose to be part of this reality by achieving expanded states of consciousness, becoming aware of the presence of God within us, relating to the whole creation as an inseparable part of it, and feeling a complete oneness with it. Dr. L.P. Masters writes,

> The knowing and experiencing of God's Presence
> is the greatest of all human experiences, as well

DISCOVER THE ETERNAL YOU!

as the most profound knowledge a person may possess. Down through recorded history, people have claimed to have experienced God's Presence. Mystics through the centuries have had visions, which they say have either given them the fullness of God's Presence experienced, or at least such inspired visionary glimpses of the divine as to suggest that the sum total of glimpses is the Presence of God. Experience of this kind is extrasensory in nature. (Masters Vol 4: module35, on line)

Higher Levels of Conscious Awareness

Higher conscious awareness is about the mystical awareness of our absolute oneness with God. It cannot be reached by either perception or conception or by any other intellectual knowledge. Instead, it is defined by the inspiration and the feeling that our connection with the divine brings us.

The physical body locks us into a frequency range or a lens through which we perceive the reality of the physical world only. When we perceive our physical world through our five senses, we normally react automatically to our perceptions based on our preconceived ideas and our memories instead of responding consciously to each perception each time.

According to the concept of higher consciousness, the average, ordinary human being goes through life only partially conscious of his eternal soul. People who consider this perceived physical reality to be their only truth are considered to be asleep and living in the confusion of this life. They are unaware of the reality of a higher dimension and the experience of an infinite consciousness, so they are not searching to discover it.

The quality of our thoughts and emotions feed and shape our consciousness. If our body and our brain are not contaminated by too many material ideas and philosophies, we can become an access point to the basic life energy in the Universe, to higher levels of consciousness or to God.

It is very important to understand the importance of achieving higher levels of conscious awareness for our personal insight and for the awakening of the "Christ" within.

When we achieve higher levels of consciousness, when our consciousness is transformed and our awareness is expanded, higher energy flows through us and unites us with the divine. Our perception of everyday life changes, and we experience the presence of the divine in our life. It lights our path and guides the choices we make by working through our intuition. Jesus said, "Know the truth, and the truth shall set you free" (John 8:32). This enormous spiritual mystery and truth exists within every living soul and within the unconscious of every human being. It is the Kingdom of Heaven within.

How to Develop Higher Consciousness?

Higher levels of consciousness exist in a dormant state in the unconscious of all men and women. It is that state of consciousness in which humans are ready to experience the state of God-centered lives which is without a beginning or an end, where "alpha and omega" are condensed into the one eternal moment of time, the "now."

Alpha and omega are the first and last letters of the Greek alphabet and a title of Christ and God in the Book of Revelation. Jesus stated, "I am the beginning and the end" (Revelation 1:8, 21:6, 22:13).

In order to develop and experience the higher consciousness and obtain the direct and blissful access to the mystery and power we call God; we need to keep our intellect still and focussed on Christ at all times. We need to leave behind our personal selves and only be aware of our universal selves. We need to develop a new level of awareness and consciousness that can become a part of the Christ Consciousness. That is what apostle Paul meant, when he said, "It is no longer I who live but Christ who lives in me" (Galatians 2: 20).

The question that often people ask me is "How do we do that and still survive physically in this life?" We do that by not ignoring our spiritual self in favor of our physical self, by living in this world but not being part of it. In other words, we achieve that by living mindfully while working for a living, by acting consciously at all times, by practicing awareness, by becoming quiet, and by meditating each and every day.

If we do not suppress our ego, it will become the driving force behind our actual behaviour instead of the presence of God. Our ego will engage our brain to produce thoughts or voices, true or untrue, to which our body will immediately react, producing either positive or negative emotions. These emotions, in their turn, will reinforce the ego and its self-created thoughts, causing harmful verbal or bodily actions in us. That will initiate a vicious, negative circle of subjective chain reactions in our minds, which will keep directing our lives, day and night.

We should be transfigured as apostle Paul said, trying to encourage people to seek the "Alpha and the Omega" awareness reality. Our egos should disappear and the word of God should live in us in order for us to become serene, joyful, inspired, and in order to even attain holiness.

We must be sure of what we believe. Most of us do not really know what we truly believe because we have not awakened the Christ within. Without the true knowledge of Christ teachings, without his foundational teaching, which are grounded and rooted in the absolute truth, a Christian cannot advance spiritually but he is destined to be limited in his or her self-consciousness.

When the Christ Mind, which was in Jesus, declared, "I am the Alpha and Omega, the beginning and the ending" (Revelation 1:8). He meant that He existed in eternity, in a state of Christ Consciousness, without a beginning or an end, in the one eternal moment of time. Based on the mystical interpretation of apostles Paul's letter to the Philippians, this is what he meant, when he wrote, "Let this mind be in you, which was also in Christ Jesus" (Philippians 2: 5).

Through the intermediary of the Christ Consciousness, we can achieve Theosis, or connect to the timeless reality of

God, and live in the pure infinite Mind without any traces of our personal self or ego. God is no longer a remote doubtful reality, but a vibrant presence in our lives.

Christ Consciousness

Christ Consciousness or Christ within, is, for me personally, the most important energy to possess. It is what makes the realization of Christian agape, joy, and peace possible in me.

Only with the mystical help of Christ within, we can free ourselves from our past and transform our state of awareness to the ultimate state of "knowing ourselves."

Eckhart Tolle, the German-born spiritual teacher and self-help author, wrote in his book *A New Earth*: "One thing we know: life will give you whatever experience is most helpful for the evolution of your consciousness. How do you know this is the experience you need? Because this is the experience you are having at this moment" (Tolle 2005).

God Consciousness or Theosis

Meister Eckhart who is a German Catholic theologian, philosopher, and mystic of the thirteenth century, said the following about God Consciousness: "The eye through which I see God is the same eye through which God sees me; my eye and God's eye are one eye, one seeing, one knowing, one loving" (Eckhart 2009).

God consciousness is a continuous remembrance that God lives in all of us and that, we are one with Him. It is a continuous awareness of the presence of God in the depth of our mind and soul. It is what guides and directs us in our daily lives.

A human being is a tiny part of the Universal Consciousness, which connects him to nature, to every other person, and to everything else which exists in the entire Universe.

Our purpose in life is to achieve God Consciousness and to be able to manifest it. The manifestation is made possible through our human consciousness, which is encapsulated in our physical body. If we manage to achieve this while we are in this material world, we will be able to receive all the available benefits from it.

When we switch our consciousness from an ego- and pride-centered consciousness to a God-Centered Consciousness, when we minimize or eliminate our personal ego, we start living our lives through the awareness of the divine presence, and we become part of the infinite, omnipotent, Universal God. We start seeing everything through God's eyes and from God's perspective; we experience an instantaneous downloading of divine energy and an awakening of the spirit within.

According to the writings of the evangelist Matthew, Jesus said, "and whosoever will lose his life for my sake shall find it" (Matthew 16:25). Based on a mystical interpretation of the above saying, "losing" means the release of our personal ego consciousness, while "finding" is the discovery of that part of our human nature where our soul and God exist as one.

Awareness of God Consciousness

The awareness of God Consciousness in us means

- that we have come to realize that we are one with the presence of God's Universal power within us,
- that God is part of our inner Consciousness,
- that we are all part of the same source of energy and strive to be conscious of this reality in our mind and soul at all times,
- that God exists through personal mystical experience,
- to believe that God, being part of us, knows exactly what our innermost thoughts, wishes and prayers are,
- that by contacting God's inner presence, we can experience physical, mental, and emotional health; divine wisdom, creativity; cosmic guidance; love; success and generally a better life.

How Do We Achieve God Consciousness?

All human beings are designed to achieve God Consciousness, irrespective of race, gender, or religious affiliation. The main reason that we cannot often exercise this potential is because we have descended into a lower state of consciousness and we are not aware of our divine potential.

"The Kingdom of Heaven within" of which Jesus spoke of many times, refers to the love and the light of God which abides within every human being beneath one's personality, beneath one's ego, behind the roles one plays in society. It is the divine spark that we all have inside us that compels us to turn to God like a magnetic needle of the compass, which always turns to the north pole. It is our deep wish to make a conscious union with our creator.

God is closer to us than we think. He is guiding us and protecting us continually. Even if we can't see the hand of the Divine right now, we must stay sure that we are connected to It and that we keep being guided by It. All we have to do is to try to feel God's presence, listen to Him, and to ask for His help.

To achieve God Consciousness, we have to know ourselves and trust in ourselves. We have to have the conscious awareness and the understanding that God exists in every one of us and that whatever we do to ourselves, or to somebody else, or to Nature as a whole, affects everyone and everything else. We all need to go through a personal change and a transformation within ourselves in order to become better, more peaceful, more compassionate people serving each other through truth and understanding.

In the teachings of esoteric Christianity found in the Philokalia and in the writings of the Fathers of the Dessert of the third and fourth centuries as well as in the writings of St. John of the Cross (John 1542-1591) we can find guidance and exercises for Christian devotees who wish to enter into a mystical union with God and for experiencing Theosis and holiness.

Causes and Effects of God Consciousness

When we, human beings, become consciously aware of the power that exists inside our mind, we actually activate

God's omnipotent and creative powers to start working on our behalf and for our benefit. The spiritual realization that we are forever one with God's presence and grace within us frees us from the problems and the sufferings of this life and fulfills the Divine will within us.

The presence of God at the innermost center of our unconscious is ready at all times to step up to the conscious level of our mind and take over our life. When this happens, we feel that we are not alone and that we all share the same source of energy throughout the Universe.

The more we are one with God Consciousness, the more effective our prayers and our healing abilities become. Our souls remain connected to the Universal whole at all times, elevating us to our natural state of grace, love, and unity. Once this is achieved, the frequency of our rate of vibration increases to such an extent that it enables us to reach different non-physical dimensions where no space and no time exists but where everything is pure energy.

Unfortunately, often people do wait until challenges come up in their lives, until their heart has been broken to the things of this material world, before they open up their heart into the higher worlds. They are dormant until they realize their temporary earthly existence before they tap into the realm of greater awareness.

Conscience

Our conscience is the centre of our esoteric world. It is the inner centre through which we come into contact with our Creator. It is an inner feeling or voice, which acts as a guide to our behaviour. It helps us determine between right and wrong and from acting upon our most basic urges and desires. It is what makes us feel guilty when we do something bad.

There are different grades of conscience. There is a conscience which is sensitive and familiar with the adoration of the living God, but there is also the corrupt conscience, which has been branded by the flame of sin.

According to St. Paul's letter to Timothy, lying and being hypocritical cauterize our conscience (1 Timothy 4:2). Also, according to St. Paul's letter to the Ephesians, losing all sense of shame and practicing every kind of impurity sears our conscience too (Ephesians 4:19).

Man has been called to follow any course he chooses. He may use his autonomy and follow either the path of righteousness or the path of evil. He thinks that he is free, but he is the servant of his passions.

It is not easy for a man to acquire a conscience of righteousness. Our conscience is easily susceptible to bad or incorrect information, to rationalization, to justification, and to all of sort of distortions coming from the popular culture around us or from within us.

Each person must act according to his or her own conscience. For a Christian, conscience needs to be formed in accordance both to reason and to what is found in the Scriptures or in the Church's interpretation of the Scriptures the under the guidance of the Holy Spirit. For a Buddhist, on the other hand, conscience is one's self-awareness. It manifests as unselfish love for all living creatures and as being one with a single whole.

CHAPTER FIFTEEN

"Theologians may quarrel, but the mystics of
the world speak the same language."

Meister Eckhart

MYSTICISM

The word "mysticism" is derived from the Greek word "μυστικός" (mystikos). It refers to the intimate contact and union of the human mind with the Divine Mind within.

Mysticism is about developing an esoteric state of total harmony with everything in the Universe. It is about developing a personal relationship with God and the Universe by reaching a higher level of conscious awareness. It is an attempt to draw near God, not by rites or ceremonies but by inward disposition.

Albert Schweitzer, a German theologian, musicologist, writer, humanitarian, philosopher, and a physician of the early twentieth century said, "All profound world-view is mysticism, the essence of which is just this: that out of my unsophisticated and naïve existence in the world there comes, as a result of thought about self and the world, spiritual self-devotion to the mysterious infinite will which is continuously manifested in the Universe" (Schweitzer 1923). In other words, mysticism starts when we are able to perceive the difference between the natural and the supernatural, between the temporal and the eternal.

Who Is a Mystic?

The mystic is a seeker who searches for his inner individual experience of the Divine, while the religious person is a believer who occupies himself with dogmas and catechism as a stepping stone to mysticism.

Some people have a natural, innate urge and tendency to search for a mystical union with God. For some, though, it is a long process that needs effort, goodwill, and persistence.

The goal of a mystic is:
- to accomplish an engagement with the Universal Intelligence,
- to gain a better understanding of the physical and metaphysical laws of Nature,
- to achieve more success in his life, better control of his fate, higher inner peace, improved health, increased happiness, and amazing joy through faith, prayer, and meditation.

Achieving the State of Mysticism

The achievement of a mystical life should be the normal outcome in the life of every Christian who has faith, prays and meditates. It is the baptismal right of each Christian and the natural result of faith, hope, and love as taught in the Christian faith.

The aim of practicing mysticism is to achieve the inner transformation of a person, which eventually leads to the inner experience of revelation, to the inner treasure house of beauty, and to the universal love and peace.

Critical and central to a mystical experience in our lives is our ability to empty our minds of all external thoughts and our ability to point our attention and of all our energy on to the one focal point of the presence of the divine within ourselves. Setting the mind on trivial things is considered by the mystics to be a waste of the power of our thoughts.

The state of mysticism can only be experienced when we sit still and our minds settle. Nobody knows when and why it happens. It often occurs in certain people as a strong and overwhelming sensation, in which their personal identity is transcended. The individual feels to be one with the whole Universe, being in full inner harmony with everyone and everything, and not a stranger living in it.

My Mystical Experience

It was almost, five o'clock in the morning. I was in Hawaii. It was one week, after the death of one of my best friends. I could not sleep. I got up and went to the patio. Dawn was just breaking. There was a deadly silence around me. I started praying, trying to center my prayer, to get closer to God.

After a while, when I opened up my eyes, I felt so humbled at heart and peaceful in mind. I had completely lost any sense of self. I was lost in the beauty of the ocean and the colours of the trees around me. I became intensely aware of the different flowers, the shape of the leaves, the movement of the ocean, and the uniqueness of the patterns of the waves. Everything was so intense and so exaggerated around me. It was overpowering! I was definitely in a different state of heightened awareness beyond any words and beyond any reason, as if I was awakened from a dormant state. I was experiencing an overwhelming connection with nature and a sense of unity and oneness with the whole Universe. There were no emotions, or thoughts, sensations, or any sense of time or of place. There was no "I" or "ego" but a pure consciousness.

I cannot tell whether this experience had taken place in a fraction of a second or over a period of several hours. Later I realized that my consciousness had a mystical experience of merging into the divine self or of uniting with God.

Quantum Mysticism

Quantum Mysticism is a set of metaphysical beliefs and practices that seek to relate consciousness and spirituality to the ideas of quantum mechanics and its interpretations. It is trying to find evidence of the existence of God and of mystical reality in science and in empirically measurable phenomena.

Quantum Physics and Quantum Mechanics is the best theory we have for describing the behaviour of matter and energy at the level of atoms and subatomic particles. Based on the outcome of the "Double split experiment" around the year 1990, scientists discovered that the outcome of a quantum experiment could change depending on whether there is an "observer" of the experiment or not. This means that the determining factor of the behaviour of energy at the quantum level is the awareness of the observer.

Whatever the observer believed would happen, the quantum field manifested it as if the quantum world is waiting for us to decide on how it is going to behave. This may mean that consciousness plays an active role in quantum theory and that consciousness and quantum mechanics are somehow linked.

The fact that consciousness affects quantum mechanics, or perhaps that quantum mechanics is involved in consciousness, shows us that our thoughts, our attention, our intentions, motives, and beliefs produce what we wish to see, making us the masters of our life and our destiny. We seem to be the ones to decide what will manifest in form out of all the possibilities in the field.

We know that 99% of the human body is made up of oxygen, carbon, hydrogen, nitrogen, calcium and phosphorus, and some other minor elements, but that is not all. In reality, we are interacting with energy waves that form a field. We are connected to everything and everyone who is in this field, with the ability to influence them and be influenced and affected by them. This is called quantum entanglement.

Based on the theory of quantum entanglement, we become entangled with people we are connected to. This theory states that one subatomic particle can interact and communicate with another particle at a huge distance, even though there are no known means for such information to be communicated. This is what Albert Einstein called "spooky actions at a distance".

CHAPTER SIXTEEN

"Faith consists in believing when it is beyond
the power of reason to believe."

Voltaire

FAITH

Faith is the belief that there is a nonphysical, spiritual dimension, an invisible world, which lies beyond and above the seen world. It is a world that is not perceived by our five senses and which is responsible for everything that takes place within it. It is the conviction that there is a purpose and a reason for everything in this life, and that everything happens for the best.

Faith allows us to accept with certainty and confidence the facts that there is a higher intelligence that is working through us and through everyone else for the good of all. It makes us believe what research in quantum physics points out: that there is a nonmaterial Universe and an extrasensory force that exists in another reality and which intersects and integrates with the physical world.

Maurice Nicoll, a Scottish neurologist, psychiatrist, author, and esoteric teacher said, "Faith is a continual inner effort, a continual altering of the mind, of the habitual ways of thinking, of the habitual ways of taking everything, of habitual reactions. To act from faith is to act beyond the range of the ideas and reasons that the sense-known side of the world has built in everyone's mind" (Nicoll, Kinney 2004).

We need to believe strongly in the existence of an all-knowing God, His infinite love for us, His non-failing care, His non-judgmental forgiveness, and His ever-present blessings, in order to be able to say, "Your will be done, not my will", with confidence to our inner presence and to mean strongly every word of it as the will of our real self and that of the inner Presence in us is one.

Jesus stressed the importance of faith by saying to us, "If you have faith as small as a mustard seed, you can say to this mountain, 'Move from here to there' and it will move. Nothing will be impossible for you" (Matthew 17:20).

Intelligence and Faith.
Faith is not a matter of intelligence and it cannot be conceived through our intellect or verified through our senses. It is not limited to the visible world; It acts beyond the range of the ideas and reasons. Faith and reason complement each other, though, for the human spirit to rise to the contemplation of truth.

Nothing outside of us is ever more powerful than the power of love and faith that lives within us. We need to shift our different energies to the level of the high energy of love, of unselfishness, and of a deep sense of faith inside our soul and mind in order to see the results of our prayers and wishes.

What Does Faith Do?

Faith opens up our inward eye, the eye of the soul, and fills it with the presence of the divine spirit. In this age of disbelief in which we live, we desperately need faith to apprehend the sacred in the midst of the ordinary daily life.

Faith is a very powerful positive thought. It is the single most important tool in our life. It is the force that draws us towards the Divine. Through faith, we transcend our human consciousness. We are led to the experience of the Christ level of consciousness and to God Consciousness. Thus, we are enabled to get access to the different attributes of God and to let the higher energies flow into and throughout our bodies. Apostle Paul, in his second epistle to the Corinthians, said, "For we walk by faith, not by sight" (2 Corinthians 5:7). In other words, we do not go where we see but where we are guided. The stronger our faith is, the greater our spiritual conscious awareness will be and the closer to God we will feel.

Having a lively faith in God helps us restrain from the external temptations, thoughts, and stimulations received through our five senses.

Faith causes our prayers to be heard and healings to be achieved, as it brings us closer to God. Our health and happiness depend on the degree of faith we carry, the love we share and the compassion we feel.

CHAPTER SEVENTEEN

"There is a mighty lot of difference between
saying prayers and praying."
John G. Lake

PRAYER

In my parents' house, we had a special prayer room dedicated to God, filled up with icons of Jesus, the Virgin Mary, saints, and angels. I was encouraged to go in there any time when I felt the need to talk to God.

Later, when I grew up and started looking for logical explanation on how things work, I realized that prayer is a thought force which, when focused in the right direction, becomes the most powerful tool a human being can possess. It is the path to communion with God, to mystical experiences, to spiritual development, and to absolute happiness and bliss in life.

Jesus spoke about the power of prayer. He told his followers, "For everyone who asks receives and the one who seeks finds, and to the one who knocks it will be opened" (Mathew 7:8-9).

In traditional exoteric prayer we ask, we seek, and we petition God. In real esoteric prayer, we seek union, oneness, and merger with God. We do not seek the things of this world. We realize that if we are in contact with the Universal Creative Power, our needs will be taken care of. Apostle Paul writes to the Philippians: "Do not be anxious about anything, but in every situation, by prayer and petition, with thanksgiving, present your requests to God. And the peace of God, which transcends all understanding, will guard your hearts and your minds in Christ Jesus" (Philippians, 4:6-7).

Our prayer can be visualized as a ladder to God in the form of a flow of energy originating in our souls. It is the opening of our mind to the highest power in the Universe; it is the communion with God through some positive words, affirmations, and thoughts of a mystical nature for the purpose of keeping attuned to the higher Mind of God and of learning to listen to the voice of the presence. God is deep within us, but we must go beneath the surface of our mind to experience His Universal Power.

Two Kinds of Prayer

There are two kinds of prayer: the esoteric and the exoteric. They both help to warm up the heart and the soul of a person and to bring one closer to his Creator. The esoteric prayer is the inner, the silent, or the mystical, while the exoteric prayer is the outer, or the obvious.

When our prayer is clear and not self-centred, when it is for the good of all, when our conscious or mental part of our mind is attuned and working with the inner truth of God's presence, when we ask for something that is according to His will, God will always respond! Jesus promised his disciples that whatever they would ask the Father in His name, it would be given to them (John 14:14).

The repetition of a prayer or the recitation of a mantra help us to eliminate the channel or groove in our mind through which repetitive occurring negative thoughts operate. By doing so and by replacing the continuous flow of negative thoughts with the positive vibrational frequency of the prayer or the mantra, we will be able to return to our true essence. Repeat a prayer like "Jesus Christ, Son of God have mercy on me" or a confirmation like "I am divine".

The answers to our prayers may not always be what we really want to hear or receive, but they will always be in our best interest. Have you heard the expression, "Thank you God for prayers not answered"? It expresses gratitude to God for not answering prayers which were not in our best interest.

A very good example of prayer not answered is given to us by Hazrat Inayat Khan, an Indian professor of musicology, a poet, philosopher, and pioneer of the transmission of Sufism to the West, wrote the following poem:

"I asked for strength,
and God gave me difficulties to make me strong.
I asked for wisdom,

and God gave me problems to learn to solve.

I asked for prosperity,

and God gave me a brain and brawn to work.

I asked for courage,

and God gave me dangers to overcome.

I asked for love,

and God gave me people to help.

I asked for favours,

and God gave me opportunities.

I received nothing I wanted.

I received everything I needed"

(Khan 1903).

For our prayers to be powerful, effective and fulfilled, they must not be just simply recited; but they must be felt inside our heart. They must be loaded with emotions of faith, love, joy, and enthusiasm and they must be expressed with the right attitudes of humility and confidence. Jesus said, "But the greatest among you shall be your servant. For those who exalt themselves will be humbled, and those who humble themselves will be exalted" (Matthew 23:11-12) and also "Therefore, whoever takes the lowly position of this child is the greatest in the Kingdom of Heaven" (Matthew 18: 4).

Any form of pride derived by self-perception of righteousness or of higher intelligence, of greater learning, of superior position, of more wealth, of better looks, etc., is a toxin to the spirit, and it creates obstacles in the path of prayer.

An Event at The United Nations

A while ago, during a United Nations celebration of forty years of being in existence, Mother Theresa being fully aware of the fact that one of the rules of the United Nations is "no prayers", she marched to the podium and she said, "We have gathered together to thank God, for 40 years of the beautiful work that the United Nations have put in for the good of the people, and as we begin the year of peace, let us say the prayer; you have all got one; we say the prayer together for peace. "Works of love are works of peace." We say it together so that we may obtain peace, and God can give us peace, by uniting us together (Mother Teresa, 2022).

Best Prayer

The best way to contact God is through prayer and through meditation in silence, in humility, in goodness, and especially in absolute love and compassion. Turn away from the outer to the inner self and to the silence of the within; try to make a conscious union with God, try to become one with His power; and realize that His power is available to us to use at all times. Pray, and do not let despair enter into your mind. Whatever a situation may be, always place it in Christ's holy hands. Praising God constantly, chanting hymns, reading the Bible, occupying ourselves with godly principles and truths opens up a tremendous possibility of success and fulfillment in our lives. Apostle Paul declares "Devote yourselves to prayer, keeping alert in it with an attitude of thanksgiving" (Colossians, 4:2).

Devotion to God and serving others with humility are the emotional ways of uniting our soul with God. Make the connection with the Father in secret and in deepest silence. Mental prayer and deep devotion, create the right conditions for the grace of God to reach us and for his power to flow through us in order to fulfill our every need.

Take your time to be with Christ every day in a quiet place where God can be heard. If we live each moment with a prayer in our heart, we transcend this world and rise above it. We rise above the darkness that is contained in this world, and we sense the light of Christ that surrounds us.

Jesus promised his Holy Spirit to his disciples before he left this world. He said, "If you love me, keep my commands. And I will ask the Father, and He will give you another advocate to help you and be with you forever— the Spirit of truth" (John, 14: 15-17). This promise confirms to us that we are not alone and that He will always be here for us, as long as we ask for His help, as long as we love Him and as long as we open our minds to Him. God will always respond, irrespective of whether His response will be what we are expecting or not.

Our prayer is heard and fulfilled, when:
- it is clear and selfless,
- it is for the good of all,
- we keep the conscious or mental part of our mind open, attuned, and working with the inner truth of God's presence,

- when we ask for something that is according to His will,
- when a mystical connection is achieved,
- when our prayer becomes part of the Universal Consciousness and we become part of "Thy will be done".

When we are in the conscious and subconscious levels of our mind and when we hear the constantly interfering voice of our ego, it is very difficult to connect with the Christ Consciousness, which leads us to God Consciousness. The more we pray using thought and words, the less we can hear the voice of the silence or the voice of God.

The successful outcome of our prayers does not depend on the numbers of the words we use, nor on how fancy our words are, nor on specific prayers given to us by other spiritually evolved people. Prayer does not need to have many impressive words. We read in the New Testament, "And when you pray, do not keep on babbling like pagans, for they think they will be heard because of their many words. Do not be like them, for your father knows what you need before you ask Him" (Matthew 6:7-8).

Quoting Dr. P.L Masters, "Many people believe in the power of prayer but is there more power in some prayers than in others? If so, which is the most powerful prayer a person can pray? The strongest and most powerful and effective prayer that one can pray is the prayer which came directly from the Christ-Mind that was in Jesus, it is the 'not my will, but Thy will be done.'" Dr. P. L. Masters adds that when we pray these words and mean every single word in our heart of hearts, then our prayer is directed to God's presence within ourselves. We let God's presence take over our body, mind, and soul. When, on the other hand, our prayers involve our personal will, which comes directly from our ego, the full potential of God's presence within us gets repressed, and its potential power is diminished (Masters 2013).

In order to see the results of your prayers, affirm your wishes quietly but strongly with faith, confidence and self-lessness. Believe absolutely in the power of God; expect the gifts of the Spirit; trust that God knows already your needs and wishes. If you wish your prayers to be answered and if you wish to attain the peace of life that leads to the libera-tion of the soul and to the love and grace of God,

- live walking a path of truth and righteousness,
- praise God,
- surrender to God's will,
- trust in the words of Jesus,
- live by His teachings,
- be kind and sharing, be humble and graceful.

Our Challenge

The darkness we experience in our life is part of the illusion-ary reality of this world we live in, which seems to grip all of us at times. The world contains darkness but it also contains light. In our own personal darkness, despair can overtake us. Our challenge during these dark times is to enter our place of prayer, to sit quietly, and to pray.

Our challenge is to close our eyes and shut out the outer world so that the eyes of our soul can begin to comprehend the true inner Light of God that is always inside us and all around us. The true Light can be hard to see with our earthly eyes. It can only be perceived by the spiritual eyes of our heart and soul.

For our prayers to be heard and answered, for our wishes to be fulfilled and for the best possible outcomes to materialize in our lives, we need to be connected to God Consciousness within. We need to stop the turmoil of anxiety-provoking, selfish thoughts in our minds. We need to fix our attention and awareness into our present state of being and surrender our mind totally to the Divine Mind. We need to let God's will take absolute control of our lives.

The more our mind concentrates on the divine through prayer and less on the false ego self, the more it is elevated to a different level of awareness. Consequently, the energy, which gets released through prayer and meditation, performs wonderful miracles, which are very hard to imagine for people who have never had the experience.

In my first book, *Above the Apparent and Beyond the Present,* I have mentioned "It has been proven repeatedly that those who pray and meditate experience an inner peace, an increase of universal love, increased patience and compassion, easier forgiveness, better health and more confidence" (Zibarras A., 2011, p.48).

Physiological changes caused by praying

According to studies conducted at the University of Wisconsin-Madison by Richard Davidson, the professor of psychology and psychiatry, and his colleagues, brain activity in Tibetan lama monks who are skilled in meditation has shown that the lamas' baseline of brain activity is much farther to the left of the brain than the activity of people who often have negative thoughts. People who have greater activity in the left prefrontal cortex are believed to be happier and to have a better immune system.

A prayer or a chant has sound. Sound is a frequency or a wave that travels, clashes, reflects, refracts, penetrates, and constantly interacts. Therefore, the vibration of the sound that we recite frequently resonates with our bio magnetic energy, which refers to the signals that are associated with specific physiological activity and with our life force. All our cells get filled by a Universal Energy that restores and maintains health in our cells.

Prayer reduces stress and is one of the best solutions for marital and relationship problems. When couples pray together, they grow closer to each other and lead happier married lives.

Prayer helps with everything from insomnia to neurosis and produces the best physiological responses in ill people. Prayer reduces our stress levels, slows our heart rate, and relieves our physical and psychological pains.

Be Thankful

Develop an attitude of gratitude and never underestimate the value of gratefulness. Praise God; give him thanks with all your heart for everything positive and everything negative, and for the value of both in your lives. Be grateful for all your blessings.

There are so many things to be grateful for. When Jesus healed the ten men who suffered from leprosy, only one of them came back to give thanks. Consequently, Jesus asked where the other nine were...

CHAPTER EIGHTEEN

"Quiet the mind and the soul will speak."
Ma Jaya Sati Bhagavati

MEDITATION

Meditation is the silent, non-verbal, spiritual form of prayer, which can take place daily, at any time and any place, for as long as possible. It can be done while walking, sitting, lying down, or at any time that we wish to collect our thoughts and contact God. A daily practice of meditation opens the surface levels of our minds to their deeper levels. It keeps our consciousness energy field at a high level so that even if some negative energy enters our field, its effect is minimal.

Meditation is the highest form of mystical prayer, is a very important tool for the purification of the mind. It leads us to connection with the Mind of within us. It is the ability to keep still, emptying one's mind of every external thought, feeling, and emotion and concentrating fully on only one thought or picture, or object of the infinite source, for as long as required.

Communicating with God through prayer and medita-tion is an attempt to either show our appreciation to God or to express a wish or a need. By meditating daily, a person's intuitive or extrasensory awareness is heightened. Intuitions, inspirations, and creative ideas come from a higher source beyond and outside the capacity of the intellect. Without meditation and the increased conscious awareness, the human mind is left only with the intellect to guide its way.

Many famous and successful people do recognize the fact that their achieved success has not been a matter of intel-ligence or of timing but it was due to being at the right place, at the right time, with the right person because of the inter-vention of a higher power.

Meditation Process

One can start meditating by taking a few deep breaths and by focusing on breathing. When we focus on our breathing, we use the breath as an object of concentration and medita-tion. Breath, which is the connecting link between matter and energy, as well as consciousness and mind, leads us to higher consciousness levels.

Say a short prayer before and after meditation. Pray before meditation to ask for divine blessing and guidance; pray at the end of the meditation to give thanks and to ask for the divine blessing for the rest of the day. Chant a hymn or meditate by repeating God's name. We can meditate on the topic of Jesus by placing Him in the centre of our mind, focusing on His image, identifying with Him, and holding on to the feeling of His presence for as long as possible. This is done to increase our mystical union with Him.

Try to repeat the infinite name of God with every breath you take until, eventually God's name becomes so strong in your consciousness that you become a living vibration of his name. When you feel those vibrations in every part of yourselves, you develop a deep connection with the infinite Light. You enter into absolute union with the only infinite power of the Universe, thus achieving absolute bliss, inner calmness, and God's guidance through life's trials and hardships.

The repetition of a prayer or the recitation of a mantra helps us eliminate the often-continuous flow of negative thoughts. It replaces those with the positive vibrational frequency of the prayer or the mantra, which flows throughout our body.

Another way of meditating is by expressing our devotion to God and glorifying his holy name, by chanting hymns, reading the Bible, and by occupying ourselves with godly principles and truths until we create a unity between body, mind, and soul. Thus, total harmony inside and outside of ourselves is established. This brings us closer to God Consciousness and the realization of our blessings.

Instead of asking God for things to be given to us, we should rather concentrate on praises, devotion, love, and appreciation. We should be fully alive and alert, appreciating the beauty of creation and accepting each moment as it comes.

Effective Meditation

For our meditation to be the most effective, it needs to be carried on, at least twice daily, morning and evening for at least fifteen minutes.

Even when you are surrounded by people and during activity, try and hold your attention on your body and your breath. When you lie down to sleep, continue being aware of your total body and your breath until you fall asleep. This will deepen your consciousness and your sleep will become more beneficial to your body and mind.

Lie flat on your back with your arms at your side, palms downward or with your arms across your stomach and your legs out straight. Relax completely with closed eyes and do the normal process of meditation until you fall asleep. If you find that lying on your side is more conducive to sleep, then lie in that position. If you do wake up during the night, keep on doing the same until you fall asleep again. When you wake up in the morning, put your awareness on your body and breath. This practice is very helpful when you are ill, as it stimulates the healing process.

Through the observation of our body and focusing on our breath, we develop the ability to separate our real selves from the objects around us while we are aware of them without clinging to them.

Mass meditation takes place in churches and other places of worship. It creates a very strong current or vibration, which connects us with the Universal Mind. This connection helps us to change our state of consciousness and to cut through our egos more effectively. It helps us become loving, kind and compassionate to the needs of others. Thus, we gain spiritual maturity that results in our realization that the key to happiness is within ourselves.

Breathing During Meditation

"Life starts with a breath and ends with a breath," Yogi Bhajan said, (Zibarras A., 2011, p.50). Concentrating on our breathing or bringing our attention to our breath is all about creating a physical and mental equilibrium as well as inner harmony.

Most people breathe 20,000 times on average, daily. Rhythmic, abdominal breathing provides us with adequate oxygen necessary to restore the body. As we inhale, we become more energized, as we exhale, more relaxed. Use your breathing as a mindfulness tool as a reminder of the present time and the value of the moment.

The meditation process has four progressive stages related to breathing, which should last for five minutes each. In the first stage, stay focused on your breath. For example, count one, after the first out-breath, then breathe in and out and count two and so continue, until you count up to ten. Then start again at one. In the second stage, concentrate on the rhythm of your breaths. In the third stage, stop counting and just watch the breath as it comes in and goes out. In the final stage, let your focus shift. Pay attention to the subtle sensation on the tip of your nose where the breath first enters and last leaves the body.

Gratitude

Give thanks to God and develop an attitude of gratitude. The more we express our thanks and appreciation to God for our blessings, the more our consciousness gets filled with divine presence and the more receptive we become to even more blessings.

Words of appreciation, which come from our personal ego consciousness and not from our universal identity are another expression of the dualistic divide in the human mind. What is of ultimate value is when the appreciation is expressed from God's presence in our mind.

St. John the Chrysostom, an important father of the early Christian Church and the author of *The Divine Liturgy* is known for his preaching and his denunciation of abuse of authority by both church and political leaders. He mentions in *The Divine Liturgy* "It is proper and right to sing hymns to You, bless You, praise You, thank You, and worship You in all places of Your dominion;" and also "You brought us into being out of nothing and when we fell you raised us again… For all these things, we thank You and Your only begotten Son and Your Holy Spirit: for all things that we know and we do not know, for blessings seen and unseen that have been bestowed upon us" (*The Divine Liturgy* 2002, p26).

Effects of Meditation

The experience of meditation cannot be described in words as it is beyond any word description. During meditation one is in one's natural state, which is the state of simple, pure consciousness.

When we meditate, we get in touch with God's universal love, which permeates right through our whole body and is projected through us to everyone else who is in contact with us. Our whole attitude and our words radiate the love of God.

A silent period of meditation at the beginning of each day relaxes us mentally and physically; it brings us into direct contact with the greatest creative power of the Universe and inspires us. Daily meditation on the divine presence transforms our consciousness to a higher level of awareness. It increases our intuitive levels and leads us to a more virtuous and inspired life, with more compassion and love towards those around us. Creative ideas thoughts, feelings, and impressions appear in our mind's awareness to be used in the physical world. Meditation provides us with intuitive wisdom and guidance as to how to minimize negative energy and how to restore the energy balance within our psycho-physical being, thus restoring serenity in our nervous system.

Studies show that experienced meditators who can achieve the deepest levels of meditative states can to tap into dormant levels of brain processes and gain more intelligence, creativity, and success in life. It has been said that many of history's greatest inventors, philosophers, and scientists received their revolutionary new ideas during their daily meditation sessions. Our higher consciousness knows much more about life than our intellect. This helps us make better decisions in life and in business and be more successful.

We should also meditate, whenever we find ourselves in any difficult or uncomfortable situation. Prophet Jeremiah wrote "Then you will call on Me and come and pray to Me and I will listen to you. You will seek Me and find Me when you seek Me with all your heart" (Jeremiah 29:12-14).

When our period of meditation is over, we need to try and keep being aware of our body and our breath during whatever activity we are engaged in such as work, conversations with others, or any physical activity.

Physiological Effects of Meditation?
Science, with the aid of advanced brain scanning technology, has proven that daily meditation increases our attention span; it improves our memory, our attention, and decision-making as it thickens certain parts of the brain's cerebral cortex responsible for the above functions (Hamblin 2013).

Those who meditate feel healthier as their breathing becomes more rhythmic, their blood pressure drops and their heart rate slows down. They enjoy longer life spans by reducing and even reversing disease and by being more relaxed and less insecure. Hope and faith replace their anxieties when they reach a state of deeper awareness and understanding and when they feel the essence and the presence of God within them (Baylor F., 2021).

Sara Lazar, a research scientist at Massachusetts General Hospital, presented preliminary results in 2003 that showed that "the grey matter of twenty men and women who meditated for just forty minutes a day was thicker than that of people who did not...." (Lazar S., YouTube 2012).

In a study published in the journal *Neuroimaging*, researchers report that "Specifically, meditators showed significantly larger volumes of the hippocampus and areas within the orbito-frontal cortex, the thalamus and the inferior temporal gyrus—all regions known for regulating emotions" (University of California. Research 2009).

A Chinese physician Master Dr. Hong Liu with Paul Perry, in his book, explains how the herbal diet, exercise, and meditation practices of Qi Gong balance the body's good and bad energies. They prevent disease and achieve good health. People enjoy greater longevity and fulfill their innate potential (Liu, Perry 2008).

Psychological Effects of Meditation?

Psychologically speaking faith, prayer, and meditation increase the levels of our confidence in God and in ourselves. They give us increased peace of mind, inner security, and increased happiness as the levels of our self-esteem and self-actualization get elevated.

I would say that people, who believe in the presence of the Divine in themselves and Divine love and help, develop an extremely positive attitude. This helps them attract the best into their lives as minds are like magnets. They attract back to them the nature of their daily thoughts.

People who meditate and purify their minds through the meditation process are happier than people who do not meditate since meditation increases the brain's production of the four primary euphoric chemicals which are dopamine, oxytocin, serotonin, and endorphins. These chemicals produce the positive emotions we feel throughout the day. The production of these chemicals continue even after the meditation session is over.

Social Effects of Meditation
Being mindful makes it easier to savor the pleasures in life as they occur, helps you become fully engaged in activities, and creates a greater capacity to deal with adverse events. By focusing on the here and now, many people who practice mindfulness find that they are less likely to get caught up in worries about the future or regrets over the past, are less preoccupied with concerns about success and self-esteem, and are better able to form deep connections with others (A Harvard Health Article 2022).

Spiritual Effects of Meditation
In a spiritual level prayer, meditation, praising God, and giving him thanks, help us to connect our real true selves with the Universal Mind and to become one with the Christ and God Consciousness in us. Once the feeling of that oneness is achieved, then it is God that inspires our prayers and there is no limitation to the blessings that can come our way.

God answers the call of each one of us who meditates in his name. Vibrate the name of God steadily, every day, every hour, every minute until God's name becomes so strong in your consciousness that you can feel those vibrations in every part of yourselves. Continue this practice until you develop a deep connection with the infinite Light of God in which there is only bliss without fears that we cannot conquer and with no relationship that we cannot perfect.

Our sense and feeling of being separate from God and other creatures is nothing but an illusion based on our senses. People who have achieved the sense of higher mystical reality know that there exists only one moment of time, which is the eternity and in which past, present and future are all one and the same. Einstein has written in a letter to his friend Robert Marcus, the following,

> A human being is a part of the whole, called by us "Universe", a part limited in time and space. He experiences himself, his thoughts and feelings as something separated from the rest—a kind of optical delusion of his consciousness. This delusion is a kind of prison for us, restricting us to our personal desires and to affection for a few persons nearest to us. Our task must be to free ourselves from this prison by widening our circle of compassion to embrace all living creatures and the whole of nature in its beauty. Nobody is able to achieve this completely, but the striving

for such achievement is in itself a part of the liberation and a foundation for inner security. (*The New York Times*, 29 March 1972)

Based on this elevated conscious awareness type of reality, the future has already happened. In other words, we have already received what we have needed and desired and what we have prayed for. We are now waiting to perceive its manifestation, through our senses and our reality.

Have faith in God, pray and meditate regularly. Transcend your limited personal ego and pride, which dominate your consciousness. Show traits of compassion towards others. Do benevolent acts if you wish to improve your health, happiness, prosperity, creativity, and your achievement levels.

What do the Scientist Say?

The study of meditation is no longer considered the flaky fringe of science, thanks to researchers such as Richard Davidson, a neuroscientist at the University of Wisconsin who helped to organize a session with a few monks in the foothills of the Himalayas. In 1992 he travelled to northern India equipped with electrical generators, computers and machines that could measure the electrical output in their brains.

The scientific studies with the Buddhist monks showed that meditation results in decreased activity in the parietal lobes, which are located at the top and back of the brain and which help to orient a person in time and space. There also appears to be an increased activity in the limbic system, which helps to process emotion. The theory is that a lack of parietal activity reduces the sense of self and makes a person feel there is no boundary between his or her body and the rest of the Universe.

New, more powerful brain-imaging equipment has drawn other researchers to the field, including scientists at Harvard, the University of California at San Francisco, the University of Pennsylvania and the University of Montreal.

Scientists and mystics are all trying to answer a number of intriguing questions such as "Are humans hard-wired to have religious or spiritual experiences?" "What happens in the brain when they do have these experiences?" "Is it something that non-religious people might be able to replicate with the right stimulation?" "Is the transcendent Buddhist experience, often described as feeling connected to everyone and everything in the Universe, the same as Christians' *unio mystica*?" "Can religion and spirituality make people healthier, as some studies suggest"?

Falling Asleep During Meditation

It is normal to fall asleep while meditating, since meditation relaxes both body and mind and moves our consciousness inward. Our body is used to falling asleep when the brain activity reaches a certain point.

In deep meditation after a while, though, we should be able to naturally move into a so-called "conscious sleep" state during which although we are asleep, we do continue to be conscious and aware of the self but not of our body or our surroundings. The state of conscious sleep, which is considered to be a form of deep meditation can be achieved in a non-REM sleep.

Mystical Experiences During Meditation

People who have been practising meditation for a long time profess that when they learn to meditate correctly and manage to reach a state of deep focal concentration, different kinds of sounds are heard in their ears like the sounds of a church bell and different coloured lights manifest within their forehead, in between their two eyebrows.

In the beginning the light starts as a tiny little white bright light. Although white and yellow lights are the most commonly experienced, one may notice that when their eyes are closed, different coloured lights as red, blue, green, even mixed lights flashing.

After some months of steady and correct meditation, the size of the light increases and one is able to see a full blaze of white light, larger than the sun. The duration and the stability of these sights increase with practice and that denotes that one is transcending the physical consciousness and dimension.

Silence

Practising silence means turning to God in the silence of our hearts and minds. It means consciously experiencing our oneness with the Universal presence which exists in all its fullness within us, around and through us. It is always available to us.

I wish to stress the importance of practising silence by saying that silence, peace and unconditional love belong to the realm where conflict and duality do not exist. When we are in ultimate union with the One, no words need to be spoken, or thoughts responded to.

We can only see the glory of God if we come to him in secret, in silence, in adoration, in the humility of our hearts and the quietness of our brains. Only, when the mind is totally quietened the absolute Presence can be known. As long as thinking occupies the mind, God cannot occupy it too. When we sense the eternal silence that is everywhere, then we sense God. "Sit still and know that I am your God" (Psalm, 46:10).

Instead of talking to God like we do when we pray, we must all get used to wait and listen for the voice of God. This voice comes not as a sound or words but as a feeling of inner knowing, as intuition, guidance, peace and joy.

The mind is like the ocean; the surface is usually turbulent but the depth is quiet. So, do not stay at the surface of your mind that is preoccupied with your worldly concerns but get into its depth, in silence.

Only in silence and in solitude, when we are alone and all the outside noise is shut down, we can be entirely free and find ourselves. More we sit in silence, the more we find that quiet place in our mind in which we can retreat. The more we can reflect on the meaning of our existence and who we really are, the more time we allocate to ourselves and the closer we grow to God. Father Thomas Keating, the founder of Centering Prayer said, "We pray with the door shut when without opening our mouths and in perfect silence, we offer our petitions to the one, who pays no attention to words but looks hard to our hearts" (Keating 2008, Ch.1).

When we are relaxed and quiet, and in contact with our inner being, the process of detaching from our everyday ego state of consciousness begins, and the focus of our full attention gets directed to God. When we meditate and concentrate on divine ideas of truth, love, life, and light or we focus on words that invoke the realization of God's attributes, we get connected to the source of all things.

Disengage from the everyday consciousness, sensations, thoughts and feelings. Turn inward into your minds, where you can discover the place in your consciousness where God is. Experience Him directly and discover the cause of all things. Sense the energy of life flowing through your body. Sense God and the eternal silence that is everywhere, and feel the enormous sense of peace, love and harmony.

CHAPTER NINETEEN

*"Timelessness is realizing that everything
that has ever or will ever happen already exists
simultaneously in another reality or dimension."*
Russell Anthony Gibbs

DIMENSIONS

Dimensions are different planes of existence. Each dimension has its defined parameters and constraints that are in tune with the frequency of that dimension and its own vibratory rate. The ability to function consciously and with awareness within a certain dimension depends on whether one's rate of vibration is in resonance with the frequency of that dimension.

Existing in another dimension means that we are crossing from one dimension into another within our human plane and this earthly reality. It does not mean at all that we are somewhere else, in a faraway plane.

We are all aware of the three physical dimensions that surround us daily and in which we live. Those are the dimensions of length, width, and depth of all the objects in our Universe.

We gain the knowledge that other dimensions do exist through higher states of inner consciousness and through any contact we may have with a being that is actually beyond our normal visual spectrum.

Multidimensional consciousness refers to the ability to be conscious of more than one dimension. Such knowledge may influence us positively if it helps us realize that this physical life is not the only life we live and that our life will continue after our physical body ceases to function. Such perceptions cause us to be more philosophical and realize that there is a law of cause and effect that goes beyond this lifetime.

Universal factors control the basic structure, organization, and function of all life in the Universe. Each of these factors descends into the physical world from the higher dimensions via primordial cosmic radiation. This refers to electromagnetic radiation, which fills the Universe since the Big Bang 13.8 billion years ago. This radiation in small amounts helps the evolution of mankind but in larger amounts, it can be catastrophic.

Physical Dimension

The human body is made out of 50 trillion cells. This makes us a community of living cells. Every live cell is a battery. It has a negative voltage on the inside and a positive voltage on the outside. It has 1.4 volts, which works out to a total of 700 trillion volts of electricity in the whole body.

Many people consider this physical reality to be their only reality or truth, so they go through life preoccupied with their own business and ignoring their infinite consciousness or their souls. They ignore the fact that whatever takes place in the physical dimension is just the tip of the iceberg of what happens in the Universe, in the complexity of creation and in its maintenance.

As humans, we strive continually working toward a better tomorrow that may never arrive, and then we die. We delude ourselves that we are promoting a better life by fighting for human rights and peace. Fighting for peace in the outer world will never result in peace. It will create more of what we are fighting against. The inner world is where the fighting must take place for each one of us individually.

We need inner transformation. We need to be spiritually awakened and evolved if we want a better world for everyone and for our life to have less worry, less stress, and less frustration. Potential forces, abilities, and talents in us will become awakened. We will realize that we are a greater person than we have ever imagined ourselves to be.

If we want to find health and happiness in this physical dimension, we must first realize that there is so much more to this Universe than what our five senses perceive. We need to expand our human consciousness to become aware of God's Consciousness in us and to manifest it around us. We need to get in touch with the truth that exists in our unconscious mind and come to realize the temporary illusions of our five senses. Our soul does not cease to exist at the end of this physical life on Earth. According to Dr. P.L. Masters, in his book *Mystical Insights*, a person's beingness extends into other dimensions of existence with a corresponding level of consciousness for each of those existences (Masters P., 2016, p.52).

Different Dimensions

Although human beings are multidimensional, not everyone can exist within different interdimensional realities because they are limited in their perception of higher dimensions and because the frequency of higher dimensions is outside the range of their ordinary human perception.

Our Universe has eleven dimensions which are simply the different facets of what we perceive to be reality. We, humans, have control of the first three physical dimensions in space in which time is relevant. We can move freely forwards, backwards, downwards, and upwards in this dimension. We have no control over the fourth dimension and over higher dimensions.

The eleven different dimensions are:

- Zero dimension which has no height, no depth, no length, and no width. A point belongs to the zero dimension.
- The first dimension is found in the one-dimensional objects that exist only in terms of length. A straight line is an example of the first dimension.

First-dimensional consciousness is molecular consisting of protons, photons, nuclei, minerals, atoms, water, and genetic codes. DNA is the foundation of all physical forms in the first dimension.

- The second dimension is perceived when we add height to a straight line and we make it look like a square. It is a flat dimension with only length and width but no depth. An example of objects in the second dimension is the TV and computer screens.

- The third dimension involves depth and gives all objects a sense of volume and a cross-section, e.g., the cube. A cube or a sphere are examples of three-dimensional objects.

- The fourth dimension is considered to be the dimension of time. Without the fourth dimension no events can take place and no changes can occur in this world. In the fourth dimension, we can control time and go forward and backward in time. We can live simultaneously in the past, present, and future.

- The fifth dimension as well as the higher dimensions we cannot perceive as they exist at a subatomic level. They deal with possibilities and the notion of possible worlds.

- The sixth dimension is the dimension of multiple powers and probabilities. One can take many forms in this dimension simultaneously like in the quantum world. We could travel back in time or go to different futures. We enter into the world of parallel universes which have the same beginning, like our Universe with the "Big Bang."

- The seventh dimension contains an infinite number of universes, which might have originated from different possibilities. A person living in this dimension can experience infinite forms of it and move freely in infinite universes.

- The eighth dimension is where there is no physical existence of any object according to the string theory.

- The ninth dimension is where there is the possibility of many aliens or many civilizations living simultaneously in the same place without being aware of the presence of the other and independent of each other. In this dimension, without physical form, one can move freely in time in any direction and be in any of the infinite numbers of universes.

- The tenth dimension contains infinite possibilities. A person living in the tenth dimension will have infinite powers. He will be able to control space and time. Everything possible and imaginable will be possible. It is the God-like existence dimension.

- In the eleventh dimension, everything imaginable or unimaginable is possible. There is nothing that cannot happen in the eleventh dimension. It is the dimension of the string theory.

PART SIX

The Divine Aspect

"We want to see the universe in its absolute pure, naked, perfection. We want to know its wonder. We want to know the totality of ourselves. That's done in steps and degrees and not in one day."

Frederick Lenz

CHAPTER TWENTY

"The true value of a human being can be found in the
degree to which he has attained liberation from the self."
Albert Einstein

ENLIGHTENMENT

One of the most important benefits of faith, prayer, and
meditation is that they all lead us gradually to the stage of
enlightenment, to God Consciousness, and holiness.

Enlightenment means going beyond the self and becoming aware of the profound Cosmic mysteries, as they relate
to human life. It means being a pure consciousness disconnected from everything material in this life and living the
synthesis of God, of Mind, and the Universe.

Enlightenment is not a state that we can acquire or
possess or understand through our intellectual abilities. It is
a connection that can be achieved and a relationship with
God to be developed. Our intellect only helps us to collect

the data and knowledge we need, to feel and experience enlightenment through our emotional centres.

Enlightenment is within each person, waiting to be discovered. It is the zenith of any practical application for life improvement as it moves us away from our spiritual darkness towards the light of knowledge. The path to enlightenment requires observing the conditioned, illusionary self which changes continually, and realizing our true, real nature, which never changes.

Our aim should be to move beyond the physical self, beyond mere survival, and the fulfillment of our basic needs only. It should be about taking the steps towards enlightenment as being enlightened has its many rewards. It produces practical results in human life greatly affecting health, relationships, self-image, and self-esteem and it satisfies many material needs.

Each one of us is an individual expression of the oneness of being, in the masterplan of the Universe and all that transpires therein. We are unique creatures, who have never existed before and may never exist again.

To be enlightened, we need to undergo a personal transformation and see the deeper reality of things and not just take things at face value. We need to build a connection with the Universal Mind while we are still living a physical life and engaged with others in everyday activities. This is what Jesus meant when he said "to be in the World but not of the World" (John 17:14-16).

Before we experience enlightenment, we carry on with our life in the usual way; after enlightenment, we still do the same things, but our attitude and our inner resistance and struggle with events and experiences change, because we realize their illusionary nature.

When we get enlightened, we become aware of our true selves, of the timelessness of our consciousness and the indestructibility of the energy in us. We see the presence of God in each other. We make a positive difference in the world we live in and in the life of all the creatures around us. We can offer peace, meaning, and hope, where there is fighting, pain, and despair.

We live in the mystical reality of the present moment in which the future has already happened. We are just waiting for it to still manifest to our five senses, in this earthly plane.

Without having experienced the blissful state of enlightenment, we are going through life in a state of sleep. We are living under the influence of our self-created thoughts, attitudes, beliefs, and assumptions which we normally adopt from our culture, our family, and society at large.

Try to broaden your focus and take your awareness away from anything material, as much as possible. Focus your awareness on nothing but space and on the invisible field of energy called the quantum field, that exists beyond this time and space. Start to feel the oneness and the wholeness of your being.

Be enlightened and feel connected to something greater which is the eternal now and you will experience the mystical reality of expanded states of consciousness. You will become conduits for the manifestation of the divine in your lives. A communion between yourselves and God will be established to the point of the ultimate union called theosis.

CHAPTER TWENTY-ONE

"Holiness requires continual effort on our part and continual nourishing and strengthening by the Spirit."
Jerry Bridges

HOLINESS

The subject of sanctification or attaining holiness should occupy the minds of all Christians. Peter, the apostle of Jesus Christ, wrote "But just as He who called you is holy, so be holy in all you do, for it is written 'Be holy, because I am holy'" (1 Peter 1:15-16).

Sanctification, which is the state of being full of the presence of God or the Holy Spirit in us at all times, is a progressive work. Someone may go to great lengths and yet never reach true holiness. He may be righteous, have much knowledge, show zeal for certain religious matters, be moral and respectable, know the scripture, keep all the commandments and yet never see the Lord as these things alone do not constitute holiness.

Although holiness may never be attained, it should always be aimed, as true holiness is a great reality. It is something that can easily be distinguished in a man. It can be felt by everyone around him. If it exists, it will show itself, as it cannot be hidden.

We cannot reach the stage of holiness by ourselves but only by the grace of God. Holiness is His special gift to His believing people. It can only be achieved if it is according to God's will. Apostle Paul wrote, "This is the will of God, even your sanctification" (1 Thessalonians 4:3), and again "By grace you are saved through faith and that not of yourselves, it is the gift of God: not of works, lest any man should boast" (Ephesians 2:8, 9).

So, what is holiness? what are the main features of a holy man and how can holiness be achieved? Holiness follows enlightenment, which follows God Consciousness. It is the outcome of being of one mind with God, living by the standard of His word, doing His will, loving His ways, and by having a great fear of displeasing Him.

The aim of a holy man is:

- to walk in love with the divine, to be humble and forgive others,
- to follow after meekness, gentleness, and patience,
- to seek the praise of God and not the approval of men,
- to offer charity and brotherly kindness with a spirit of mercy and benevolence towards others,
- to avoid all lying, backbiting, cheating, dishonesty, and unfair dealing,
- to live with spiritual mindfulness.

Why holiness is important?

Holiness is very important because it is our only way to salvation. It is the end and the purpose for which Christ came into the world. "Without it no man shall see the Lord" Apostle Paul writes (Hebrews 12:14).

For Christians, Christ is the beginning of all holiness. The way to be holy is to come to Him by faith, embrace Him, and be united with Him. Holiness comes from Christ solely and it is the end result of our vital union with Him or of the state of Christ Consciousness. It is the fruit of being a living branch of the "True Vine".

A holy Christian man will strive to be like our Lord Jesus Christ. He will live a life of faith in Him. He will draw all his daily peace and strength from Him. He will also try to have the mind that was in Him, and as apostle Paul wrote, he will be "conformed to His image" (Romans 8:29).

When we achieve holiness, we abide in Christ. Jesus said "Abide in Me and I in you, he that abides in Me and I in him, the same bears much fruit" (John 15:4,5).

CHAPTER TWENTY-TWO

"One encounter with Jesus Christ is enough
to change you, instantly, forever."
Louis Palau

JESUS THE CHRIST

"My Jesus, I love You above all things and I desire You in my heart. As though You were already there, I embrace You and I unite myself wholly to You. Permit not that I should ever be separated from You" (Catholic Mass, Loretto Abbey).

Etymologically, the word or the title "Christ" comes from the Ancient Greek word "Christos,"which means the "Anointed One" or the Messiah.

Talking in the deepest Christian terms, we can call Jesus the Christ, the "Logos", the Word of God, a term which in itself suggests the idea of the Cosmos being perceived as a theophany or a self-revelation of God. Jesus is also called Emmanuel, meaning "God with us". He is the son of God, the son of man, the savior of the world. His teachings are associated with miracles, peace, love, forgiveness, and healing. St. Paul wrote in his letter to the Romans "the invisible things of Him from the creation of the world have been seen, being understood by the things that are made, even His power and Godhead…" (Romans 1:20).

Who is Jesus Christ?

Jesus has been acclaimed as the greatest religious leader in the world and as the most influential spiritual figure to have lived on our planet. He is the incarnate word of God, which became flesh and dwelt among us. "We have seen his glory, as of the only son from the Father, full of grace and truth" (John 1:14).

Jesus, followed by His disciples, traveled through Judea and Galilee, teaching and guiding His followers. He taught the multitudes, by using parables and stories, which helped people of His times understand what He wanted to say about God and the nature of our salvation.

Parables added a new dimension to the oral and written tradition of the Hebrews. They described an allegorical story that conveyed a moral principle, a spiritual lesson, or a universal truth. The most well-known parables are that of a woman searching for a lost coin, of the sower sowing the seeds, of a farmer concerned about the weeds in his farm, of the return of the prodigal son, the parable of the mustard seed, the fig tree, the lilies in the field and many others.

Jesus explained only to His disciples the inner esoteric teachings contained in the parables. "The people were astonished at His doctrine; for He taught as one having authority, and not as the scribes" (Matthew 7:28-29).

Although, many of Jesus' original teachings have been removed, changed, misinterpreted, or replaced by doctrines that are often in almost opposition to what Jesus has taught, most of Jesus' life is told through the four gospels known as the canonical gospels, written by Matthew, Mark, Luke and John.

Jesus proclaimed that He is the way, the truth, the life, and the light. He is the good shepherd, He is the vine, and He is the door. He said, "I am the way, the truth, and the life. No one comes to the Father except through Me" (John 14:6).

Jesus healed many sick, blind, and lame people. He forgave sins, He multiplied fish and loaves of bread to feed thousands on more than one occasion, He turned water into wine, He delivered the demon-possessed, He walked on water, He calmed the stormy sea, He raised children and adults from death to life.

Jesus lived a sinless life. His life was based on His superior moral teachings. He exemplified love for mankind, sacrifice, humility, purity, obedience, and devotion to God. He was not recognized as the Messiah by many during His stay on Earth because He differed from their preconceived ideas about the Messiah.

Although Jesus is no longer with us physically, as He was with his original disciples, He remains present to us in a powerful and deeply spiritual way as the risen Christ. He sends His life-giving, life-healing spirit into our lives, and by doing so He calls us into a more profound union with God.

Christ must somehow be touched by our love, by our kindness, devotion, and humility, in order to give us his grace. Thus, we will serve this humanity in humility and peace with a consciousness of self-realization. The way we look at things will change and we will be able to understand clearly the psyche of everyone and everything. "God opposes the proud, but gives grace to the humble" (1 Peter 5:4).

It is one thing to speak about Jesus' presence in us and it is something different to experience His presence as the light illuminating our path, protecting and guiding us.

Miracles Performed by Jesus.
In the New Testament texts, based on the accounts of the four evangelists, we do perceive the transfer of divine energy in the healing touch of Jesus, which was causing both physical and spiritual healing to people.

Some of the many miracles, which Jesus performed, are:
- The cleansing of the ten lepers (Luke 17:11-19),
- The healing of the mute (Mark 7:32-35),
- The healing of the blind (Matthew 9:27-29),
- The healing of the paralytic (Matthew 9: 1-8),
- The healing of the possessed man in Capernaum (Mark 1:23-26),
- The raising of Lazarus from the dead (John 11:38-43),
- The raising of the son of the widow of Nain (Luke 7:11-15),

- The raising of the daughter of Jairus, the Synagogue official (Mark 5:22-24, 38-43).

The Mystical Teachings of Jesus

Jesus was a great mystic as only a true mystic could have spoken words such as "For, behold, the Kingdom of God is within you" (Luke 17:21).

Jesus' teachings referred to our spirit, to our consciousness, to our indestructible aspect from which all states of pure love, of real joy, and universal peace emanate. Some mystics have described this as the ultimate state of existence in bliss and joy or as achieving the "Christ Consciousness" or as a "Christ within" state.

Jesus was the pure mind and essence of Christ inside the body of Jesus, which was most of the time, totally in charge of what Jesus was teaching. He said "I am the Light of the world. Whoever follows me will never walk in darkness, but will have the Light of life" (John 8:12).

Jesus came to Earth to teach us how to save ourselves by raising our state of consciousness. He taught us how to find the Kingdom of God within us. He told us that the Mind of God dwells within our minds and that the way to eternal happiness, joy, and peace is through the Kingdom of Heaven within.

Jesus' teachings were designed for people who were at different stages of spiritual development and different levels of consciousness. He addressed the individuals who wished their true selves to be awakened and enlightened. He taught them the way to get in touch with God and the Holy Spirit within as a personal experience. He also taught the higher meanings of "divine love" and "divine mercy", which transcend the confines of church walls.

Although Jesus is no longer with us, He remains present in us as the Holy Spirit, as the indwelling presence of God through the surrender of the human will to Him. When we take Jesus literally, and see His teaching from the physical dimension, we are faced with the impossible. How can we truly love our neighbor as ourselves? But when we do consider the teachings of Jesus from a higher spiritual perspective, His words suddenly make more sense.

Let us remember what Jesus has taught us. He commanded us:

- to love one another,
- not to do unto others what we do not wish others to do to us,
- to love our enemies,
- to pray for those who hate us,
- to be charitable,
- not to be hypocrites,
- to be just,
- to have clear hearts (Matthew 5:44-48).

Jesus taught that within us, we all hold, the power to love and forgive. As we learn to forgive, we give ourselves the gift of inner peace. When we forgive, we get forgiven and we free ourselves from every unwanted negative thought and feeling. "For if you forgive others when they sin against you, your heavenly Father will also forgive you. But if you do not forgive others their sins, your Father will not forgive your sins" (Matthew 6:14-15). Only forgiveness, love, and the giving up of all judgment, allow us to enter the Kingdom of Heaven.

Jesus promised us that when the true essence of His teachings enters into our hearts and influences our everyday actions and deeds, if our word is true and if truth prevails in our everyday lives, then we would be living in our highest consciousness of awareness, which is "Christ Consciousness." Hence, we will become a "God-realized person" and the grace of God will come upon us. "The Lord is with you when you are with Him. If you seek Him, you will find Him, but if you forsake Him, He will forsake you" (2 Chronicles 15:2).

Realize that you are not separate from God or Christ as you are not separate from each other. When the Holy Spirit lives in you, you can experience Christ Consciousness. Putting your lives into the hands of Jesus empowers you to hope in that mysterious promise of eternal life as you journey toward your death.

Jesus also spoke to us about criticism and judgment. He said that as we judge others, we will be judged. "Do not judge, or you too will be judged. For in the same way, you judge others, you will be judged, and with the measure you use, it will be measured to you. Why do you look at the speck of sawdust in your brother's eye and pay no attention to the plank in your eye? How can you say to your brother, 'Let me take the speck out of your eye,' when all the time there is a plank in your own eye? you hypocrite, first take the plank out of your eye, and then you will see clearly to remove the speck from your brother's eye" (Matthew 7:1-6).

We see the magnanimity of Jesus and the demonstration of His divine forgiveness and His unconditional love in Calvary, when He said, "Father, forgive them, for they do not know what they are doing"(Luke 23-34).

The Sermon on the Mount by Jesus:
The Sermon on the Mount is the most familiar section of Jesus' message. Never before had anyone heard such marvelous truths presented in such an interesting and meaningful manner like in the Beatitudes spoken by Jesus.

1. "Blessed are the poor in spirit for theirs is the Kingdom of Heaven" (Mathew 5:3).
We will be blessed if we can control our egos. Only by diminishing our egos, controlling the overflowing of thoughts and ideas in our minds, and connecting with our real inner selves, we can let the power and grace of God flow through us. The poor in spirit are those of us who think less and less about ourselves and about the need to control our lives and more about God who is first and foremost in our minds.

2. "Blessed are those who mourn, for they shall be comforted" (Mathew 5:4).
Anytime a spiritual law is broken, consequences follow, in the same manner as when physical or social laws are broken. Human errors of judgment will or purpose cause bad things to happen. Human selfishness, indifference, and stupidity are

always at the root of human misery and suffering. Sickness and disease are a lack of harmony between ourselves and our environment. For us to enjoy physical, mental, and spiritual health, we must start by mourning for ourselves and the death we brought upon ourself so that our real inner selves can be awakened through prayer, repentance, and through God's forgiveness and grace. God comforts us when bad things happen by giving us His peace and courage, hence alleviating our sorrows.

3. "Blessed are the meek for they shall inherit the Earth" (Mathew 5:5).

We will be blessed if we are emotionally stable and mature people who have reached such a state of humility and spiritual growth that nothing can disturb our peace of mind. We should be neither excitable nor depressed, but calm, kind, patient and persistent in our efforts. We should be quiet, in control of our emotions, and transparent about anything that goes on around us. To be meek does not mean to think less of ourselves but to think more of God and His infinite power over everyone and everything.

4. "Blessed are those who hunger and thirst for righteousness for they shall be satisfied" (Mathew 5:6).

Happiness does not lie in success, fame, or power, but in righteousness. It feels good to do the right ring. Real happiness is different than simple excitement. Real happiness brings tears of joy into one's eyes. It is derived from meaning, which is related to the virtues of discipline and obedience. They are both necessary for spiritual growth and peace of mind.

5. "Blessed are the merciful for they will obtain mercy" (Mathew 5:7).

When God's goodness can be seen, when His presence is not doubted by the human intellect, his mercy can be experienced by all of us. Every one of us has received so much mercy from God that we all need to be as merciful as possible to our fellow human beings. Every action in this Universe produces a reaction of equal strength. If we treat people nicely, we will be treated nicely. If we spread love, compassion, and forgiveness around us, we will encounter love, compassion, and forgiveness. If we spread happiness to those around us, we will be happy. If we make everyone, we meet feel beautiful and unique, we will be appreciated. We have to give in order to receive. This is the law of proportionate return and attraction.

6. "Blessed are the pure in heart for they shall see God" (Mathew 5:8).

We will be blessed if we manage to get rid of all negative emotions and feelings like jealousy, anger, hatred, and misery in our lives and if we adopt a healthy, positive, loving, compassionate, and kind attitude toward all of God's creation. Being positive breeds positive actions. Love turns enemies into friends. Emotional and spiritual health enables us to experience the mercy, the grace, and the presence of God. Mother Teresa wrote "We all long for heaven where God is, but we have it our power to be in heaven with him right now, to be happy with him at this very moment. But this means being: Loving as he loves, helping as he helps, giving as he gives, serving as he serves, rescuing as he rescues, being with him all 24 hours of the day, touching him in his distressing disguise" (Mother Teresa).

7. "Blessed are the peacemakers for they shall be called children of God" (Mathew 5:9).

Every one of us can be a peacemaker by doing and saying something positive and by building bridges. Being a peacemaker can be extremely difficult but rewarding especially when using the restoring power of love and when bringing Jesus Christ into human hearts.

8. "Blessed are those who are persecuted for righteousness's sake for theirs is the Kingdom of Heaven" (Mathew 5:10).

Persecution is a situation that many of us have faced or will face in the form of rejection, harassment, peer pressure, wrong assumptions, and accusations or discrimination. Emotional persecution that attacks our self-esteem and self-image can be unbearable as it often results in self-persecution and experiences of guilt and remorse. Persecution attacks both losers and winners, as it can be a result of envy and jealousy for someone's success. For us to get out of persecution as a winner and not a loser we need to be able to remain positive at all times and under any circumstances. We need to be equipped with a spiritual and emotional support system, to insist on doing what we consider to be the right thing to do, to forgive those who hurt us, to persist in trusting God, and to pray for strength and endurance.

If we live long enough in human society, sooner or later we will feel that unfairness and injustice are part of social living because we will know of someone who has treated us unfairly. We can react to the people who hurt us by hurting them back. That's the easiest and most automated response to make, in order to retaliate, no doubt about it. Jesus gave us another option; He told us to do the exact opposite. He wants us to respond in love. If we respond lovingly, to an aggressive and unjust person, that doesn't mean that we continue to allow injustice. On the contrary, we seek justice by responding in love and without violence.

How to Experience the "Kingdom of God."

Jesus once said, "Know the truth and the truth shall set you free" (John 8:32). This enormous spiritual mystery and truth exist within the unconscious of every human being. It is the Kingdom of Heaven within. It is the closeness of God in us, in our everyday lives.

The Kingdom of Heaven can be uncovered through daily meditation, which opens the inner spiritual eye. It can be experienced by the power of our faith and love, which unites us with the ultimate positive pole of God and leads us the farthest away from the negative pole from which all sickness, accident, ugliness, and unhappiness emanate.

Meditation through faith is one of the basic ways that we can come into direct contact with the divine part in us. Every time we meditate, we create inwardly an energy frequency between our self and the Universal Mind. This enables us to connect with the presence of God in our minds. Jesus said "But seek first His Kingdom and His righteousness and all things will be given to you, as well" (Matthew 6:33). This means that our wishes will be realized and our prayers will be heard and answered.

CHAPTER TWENTY-THREE

"Where mercy, love, and pity dwell,
there God is dwelling too."
William Blake

KNOW YOUR GOD

According to Albert Einstein's theories and findings, there is a definite plan and design for this Universe and for this creation as a whole. Albert Einstein declared that there has to be certain intelligence behind such a complex and intricate design. He believed that there was a divine intelligent designer and a designed plan, behind everything which is both visible and invisible to us.

There is nothing in the whole Universe but law and order. There are no chances, no coincidences. Everything happens for a reason. Therefore, there must be an intelligent force and tremendous energy and power behind it all. This spirit of this infinite energy and life force, we see in every living creature is what we call God.

God cannot be expressed nor described, as we do not have any conception of God. We cannot understand God through our intellect nor we can try to interpret everything by using our logic. It would be a futile and useless effort leading only to confusion. A finite mind cannot grasp the infinite. John the Chrysostom, the author of *The Divine Liturgy*, mentions "You are God ineffable, inconceivable, invisible, incomprehensible, existing for ever and for ever the same"...... (Greek Orthodox Mass 2002, p25).

Some people hope to find God or to feel the presence of the infinite Mind in them because they believe that they are part of God and the Universal Mind. They believe that within them abides the love and the Light of God. Alphonsus Liguori, who was a famous bishop, confessor, doctor of the church, and moral theologian during the eighteenth century, said "Your God is ever beside you indeed, He is even within you" (Liguori 2021).

We all individualize the expression of this infinite power according to our level of spiritual understanding. The fact remains that He is much closer to us than we think. Even if we cannot see the hand of the divine right now, we must be sure that we are connected with it and that we keep being guided by it. All we have to do is to try to feel his presence and listen. There is nothing that can get in between God and us except our egos, our negative attitudes, and our bad thoughts.

Intimacy with God means the realization of God's presence in our lives and the experience of God's touch which is accompanied by a sense of warmth, peace, and confidence. If we shift and transform all our energy to the high vibration of God's love energy, nothing will ever be more powerful than the love that lives within us. We will feel the presence of God within us in the form of wisdom, love, and truth much easier, when we practice a devotional attitude and humble worship rather than by any amount of mental power or intelligence.

The biblical God we read about, in the Old Testament, is just a starter kit for discovering God and entering into a relationship with him. God is expressed in the Bible with the saying "I am that I am", which according to the mystical interpretation, means that there is no past and no future in the sense of God. God just is. Jews and Christians believe that what happened 2000 years ago, is still relevant and true and it is in the "now", as earthly time is compressed in God's time.

Through our total commitment to God and through the unconditional surrender to His power, we can experience the manifestations of all the different positive attributes of God like love, healing, forgiveness compassion, wisdom, and guidance in our life. Through our intimacy with God, we can get liberated from life's illusions, we can see the divine spark in the world and we can open up a tremendous possibility of success and fulfillment in our lives.

Carolyn Myss in her book, *Entering the Castle: An Inner Path to God and Your Soul* mentions the following about St. Teresa of Avila, a Spanish nun of the 16th century, "Teresa was extremely compassionate in her understanding of how difficult it is to utter the prayer of unconditional surrender" also "Few of us can handle seeing God in everyone and in everything every minute of every day. We can visit that truth now and again… but few of our souls are strong enough to generate continuous compassion, understanding, love, non-violence, and generosity of mind and heart, words and deeds (Myss 2007, p.71).

For us to be able to experience the full high vibrations of God though, those high- frequency vibrations have to slow down for us and be reduced to a frequency that our physical beings can withstand. John Calvin, a French theologian, pastor, and reformer of the sixteenth century, said "If you want to know God come to know yourself, and if you want to know yourself, come to know God" (DeYoung 2010) (Schuller R., 2006).

If we want to know our God, we need to sink into our innermost real self and feel the presence of God by blocking our senses from external objects. We need to bring ourselves closer to God who is present in the God-centre of our mind, which is the "Holy of Holies" or the Kingdom of Heavens inside us.

In my previous book, *Above the Apparent and Beyond the Present*, I mentioned, "It is evident that for Aristotle and Plato, God is the one who is beyond the Universe, the transcendent and the perfectly self-subsistent being, the "uncaused cause", the eternal and the omnipotent. For Plato, the whole Cosmos is a theophany, in other words, a manifestation of the divine presence, the divine order and the divine Power" (Zibarras A., 2011, p 68). Also, I mentioned "We can therefore see that the idea of God did not generate out of fear in man, as many people believe it to be. If anything, fear is a negative emotion; it creates negative feelings, which move us away from God. The idea of God was generated out of deep philosophical thinking, transcendent perception, absolute reasoning and deductible evidence" (68).

Searching for God in the brain

Our ability to unite with the divine depends on how successfully we attune ourselves to it and by how much we increase the frequency of our electromagnetic vibrations to approach the frequency of the universal energy.

We can increase our rates of vibrations by working on our higher selves, having faith in God, loving the whole creation, having positive thoughts and emotion, and a selfless attitude.

In the same way, when we are in a state of fear, anger, negativity, or denial of our divine source, when we abuse our body with unhealthy food and our mind with alcohol and drugs, we are out of tune with the divine energy. Our field becomes blocked, obscure, and clouded and we can only perceive matter or energy of lower vibrations.

In the October 2007 issue of *Scientific American*, David Biello, a contemporary award-winning journalist, comments on the findings of neuroscientist Mario Beauregard of the University of Montreal as follows, "The spiritual quest may be as old as humankind itself, but now there is a new place to look: inside our heads. Using MRI and other tools of modern neuroscience, researchers are attempting to pin down what happens in the brain when people experience mystical awakenings, during prayer and meditation, or during spontaneous utterances inspired by religious fervor". And he asks the question "is there a God spot in the brain" (Biello 2007).

Such efforts to reveal the neural correlates of the divine—a new discipline with the warring titles 'neurotheology' and 'spiritual neuroscience'—not only might reconcile religion and science but also it might help point to ways of eliciting other pleasurable worldly feelings in people who do not have them or who cannot summon them at will. Because of the positive effect of such experiences on those who have them, some researchers speculate that the ability to induce them artificially could transform people's lives by making them happier, healthier, and better able to concentrate.

Ultimately however, neuroscientists study this issue of "spiritual neuroscience" because they want to better understand the neural basis of a phenomenon that plays a central role in the lives of so many. "These experiences have existed since the dawn of humanity. They have been reported across all cultures", Beauregard says. "It is as important to study the neural basis of [religious] experience as it is to investigate the neural basis of emotion, memory or language" (David Peskovitz 2007).

Proofs for the existence of God

Everything that exists has a cause therefore the Universe must have a cause too. It was caused by the first cause, which is an uncaused identity known as God.

Here are some points that can be used as proof for the existence of a single superior intelligence, which has coordinated and created the whole Universe.

1. There are similar geometrical patterns seen everywhere in the Universe and in nature indicating that there is a single Creator. The Fibonacci ratio which is the following sequence of numbers 0,1,1,2,3,5,8,13,21,34… and so on, appear in human DNA as well as in many flowers and fruits. The ratio between the Fibonacci ratio numbers points out to the golden ratio of 1:1.6, which is derived by dividing each number of the Fibonacci series by its immediate predecessor.

2. An extremely long and complex code is found inside human DNA, which is located inside the nucleus of all the cells of our body. This code is responsible for all our complex and sophisticated bodily functions and contains the genetic information inherited by our ancestors.

3. No matter by itself can create information. Information comes from intelligence. It cannot be created randomly without any intelligence behind it. Computers are instructed to perform any task using binary codes of zeros and ones. In the same way, the code that is placed inside the DNA is written in the form of the four ACTG, which is the acronym for the four chemicals of Adenine, Guanine, Thymine, and Cytokine. The different arrangements and combinations of

this acronym create different instructions in the DNA code, which is three billion letters long.

4. The most intelligent complex designs like the DNA, the cells, the atoms, the stars, the galaxies, plants, flowers, birds, insects, animals, humans, trees, and the whole Universe cannot be explained without the existence of a supreme designer, an extremely intelligent and capable Creator behind it all. This super intelligent programmer of all the living and the non-living things in the Universe cannot be anyone else than God.

5. Similar designs found at the microscopic level of atoms are observed in planetary systems. When we look into an atom, we see many electrons revolving around a nucleus in its orbit. They spin around their axis, which closely resembles the planetary system and the larger galaxies. In other words, the same signature of the same designer appears in the micro- and the macro-Cosmos.

6. The delicate balance, the connection, and the interdependency, we see in the whole Universe is an indication of one supreme coordinating power, which we call God.

7. If we look at nature, we see that we are all connected. Even non-living things have a deep connection with living things. We need other humans, animals, insects, microorganisms, trees, and many non-living things to survive. Various cycles in nature like the water cycle, carbon cycle, nitrogen cycle, and oxygen cycle indicate how everything is interconnected in nature.

8. The whole Universe acts like a huge machine made up of an infinite number of similar subdivisions of smaller machines working in perfect synchronism with each other. Each part has its function to perform. The above perfection, synchronicity, and finely tuning of the Universe again point out the existence of a super-intelligent single mind behind it all. According to the famous physicist Stephen Hawkins, if the rate of expansion in the Universe after the Big Bang, was smaller even by one part in one hundred thousand million, the Universe would have re-collapsed into a fireball to a gravitational attraction.

9. The nonphysical aspect of the human consciousness leads to the indirect evidence of God. According to research by scientists, it is impossible to explain human consciousness by the mechanisms of the brain alone; therefore, there must be a nonphysical aspect to human consciousness. Thoughts and emotions are physical processes but consciousness is not. We know that the physical and the nonphysical are linked and interconnected. This amazing interaction is only possible by an intelligent design, which needs a super designer.

10. When we observe the Universe, we see that everything living or non-living is ordered towards a purpose as if they are all guided by a superintelligence, which is pushing and moving them toward a goal. Things do not act randomly. Everything is assigned a task by a superintelligence. Sunrises and sunsets follow a routine schedule. Leaves in the plants make food for the tree through the process of photosynthesis. Cells in our bodies are synthesizing protein. Digestive

systems and respiratory systems are performing their function perfectly, even without our notice.

The above tells us that there must be a supreme power or supreme intelligence that controls and guides all objects to their final purpose. A higher intelligence must exist that regulates events in such a way that the best possible result is accomplished at all times, although we are not aware of it at any particular time.

Divine Intervention

We are intuitive beings interconnected with others in spirit. We are limited in space and time, as we are trapped in a physical body, living in a physical world. We can though, experience moments of inspiration, intuition, and of contacting the presence of God as a pure infinite light, in the spiritual level of our being.

We experience a pure awareness of the divine intervention in our earthly life when we manage to transmute our lower energy fields to higher more harmonious configurations of the energy of the divine consciousness. Consequently, when we connect to the power within, while the outer Universe stays still as an impersonal mathematical system, we can feel that our life is governed by a wonderfully orchestrated Universal Mind and that eventually, everything follows the divine plan.

The more our conscious awareness expands, the more we sense positive coincidences and intuitions expressed in the physical world. These are the God-inspired intuitions, which can be perceived through deep meditation states, chanting, and higher vibrations. The higher vibrations harmonize with even higher rates of vibration, which can access the universal realm of knowledge. Certain people can detect codes that come from higher realms of reality.

Unfortunately, studies reveal that the average human being goes through life only partially conscious of his eternal being, due to the influences of external impulses and the preoccupations of daily life. Thus, the physical body vibrates in a frequency range that enables people to perceive the physical reality, as their only reality and to go through life half-asleep instead of searching for their infinite consciousness through which they can obtain power, intuitions, and guidance.

Only when we close our physical eyes and open those of the soul, only when we are filled with nothing else than the awareness of pure consciousness, we can connect to the unlimited reality of God. Consequently, we can accept spiritual and psychic transmissions.

CONCLUSION

"All the suffering there is in this world arises from
wishing ourselves to be happy. All the happiness there is
in this world arises from wishing others to be happy."
Shantideva

I HOPE AND WISH MOST sincerely that through this
book I managed to offer a deep insight into the nature and
workings of the human mind and the universal truths. I hope
that I managed to provide an inner path to self-knowledge
and to the spiritual knowledge of God.

We all have the potential for self-transformation and
connection with the divine, as long as we know what to do
at each stage of our spiritual journey. When we consciously
become aware of the existence of God, we will come to
realize that the presence of this greater intelligence is the
only reality of our beings.

This realization will have a transforming effect on our
lives. It will teach us how to control our minds and how to

keep good motivation in our actions. It will help us become fully enlightened people and guide us to the mystical union with God or to theosis.

The realization of the two aspects of our nature, namely the real self and the illusionary self, will cause more harmony in us, in our families, and in our society in which peace and joy will prevail.

I wish to close with an appeal to all who have read this book to retain the light of Universal Awareness and to dedicate themselves to the good of humanity and its needs.

WORKS CITED

Alphonsus, Liquori. *How to converse with God*. Tan Books, 2009. https://www.goodreads.com/work/quotes/14005689-how-to-converse-with-god

Andersen, U.S. *Three Magic Words: The key to Power, Peace and Entry.* Wilshire Book Co, 1977.

Armstrong, K. *The History of God.* Ballantine Books, 1999 Aristotle. Metaphysics. Oct 8, 2000 https://www.britannica.com/biography/Aristotle/Philosophy-of-mind

Baylor, F. Research. College of Medicine, University of Wisconsin. https://www.bcm.edu/research/baylor-research

Benson, Dr. Herbert. *Timeless Healing: The Power and Biology of Belief.* New York, NY: Fireside, 1997. Print.

The Bible. Print

Biello, D. Scientific American, 2007. https://www.scientificamerican.com/podcast/episode/8f8d78a7-e7f2-99df-3a2c341cb563b8c7/

Bodanis, David. *E=MC2: A Biography of the World's Most Famous Equation.* New York, NY: The Berkley Publishing Group, 2000. Print.

Bloom, A. *The Republic of Plato.* Basic Books, 2016.

Braza, Jerry. *Moment-by-Moment: The Art and Practice of Mindfulness.* Tuttle Publishing, 1997. Print.

Cheney, Margaret. *Tesla; Man out of time.* New York, NY: Touchstone, 2001. Print.

Chidananda, Swami. http://www.chidananda.org. 2011.

Coniaris, Anthony M. *Confronting and Controlling Thoughts: According to the Fathers of the Philokalia.* Minneapolis: Light and Life Publishing, 2012. Print.

Cousens, Gabriel. *Conscious Eating.* North Atlantic Books, 2000.

DeYoung, K. *A Calvin Clarification, 2010.* https://www.thegospel-coalition.org/profile/kevindeyoung/a Calvin clarification.

Easwaran, Eknath. Seeing With the Eyes of Love: Reflections on a Classic of Christian Mysticism, Nilgiri, 1991. Print.

Eckhart. *Meister Eckhart, from Whom God Hid Nothing: Sermons, Writings, and Sayings.* New Seeds, Boston & London, 2005.

-*The Essential Writings.* Translated by R. Blakey. Harper One, *2009.* https://www.goodreads.com/quotes/7169

Einstein Albert. *On Truth and Reality. Theology: Albert Einstein, Albert Einstein Quotes on God, Religion, and Theology & Science.* Web https://awakentheworld.com/transcript/samadhi-1-maya-the-illussion-of-the-self, 2017.
https://www.goodreads.com/quotes., 2012.

Fedotov, G.P. (Editor). *The Way of a Pilgrim and Other Classics of Russian Spirituality.* New York, NY: Dover Publications, 2003. Print.

Hamblin, James. *Study: Meditation improves Memory, Attention.* Health, May 6, 2013. https://www.theatlantic.com/health/archive/2013/05/study-meditation-improves-memory-attention/275564/

Hamblin, R. *Role of religious attendance and identity conflict in psychological well-being.* Journal Article. *https://psycnet.apa. org/record/2013-23683-013*

A Harvard Health Article. Benefits of Mindfulness:Practices for Improving Emotional and Physical Well-Being. *.//www. helpguide.org/harvard/benefits-of-mindfulness.htm*-Meditation. https://www.helpguide.org/home-pages/harvard.htm. 2022

Hong Liu, Perry Paul, *The healing Art of Qi Gong: Ancient Wisdom from a Modern Master.* Grand Centra; Publishing, 2008.

Jung C.G. *Psychological reflections, A new Anthology of His Writings 1905-61,* Princeton University Press, 1973.

Jungian Centre for the Spiritual Sciences. https://jungiancenter. org/jung-on-miracles/#sdfootnote2anc

Khan, Hazrad I. https://www.spiritualityandpractice.com. 2011

Keating, Thomas. *The Path of Centering Prayer: Deepening Your Experience of God.* Sounds true, 2017.

Kellerman Henri. *The Discovery of God: A Psycho revolutionary Perspective.* Springer, 2013.

Kent C. *Place for writing thoughts.* Independently published, 2020.

Kirov Blago. Albert Einstein: Quotes and facts. Blago Kirov, 2015.

Lazar Sara. YouTube, 2012. https://scholar.harvard.edu/sara_lazar/home.

Levene L. *I Think, Therefore I Am: All the Philosophy You Need to Know.* Michael O'Mara, 2010.

Lewinson-Lenz. http://www.picturequotes.com. 2020.

Lewinson, Liz. *American Buddhist Rebel: Rama- Dr. Frederick Lenz.* Skye Pearl, 2022

Loretto, Abbey. Catholic Mass. https://dailytvmass.com

Love, Jeff. The Quantum Gods: *The Origin and Nature of Matter and Consciousness.* Authors Choice Press, 1979.

Masters Dr. Paul Leon. *Mystical Insights: Knowing the Unknown.* University of Sedona Publishing, 2016. Print.

The Theocentric Way of Life. https://university of metaphysics.com/extrasensory-contact-with-god, 2018.

Mauskopf, Seymour, Michael McVaugh. *Obituary: Joseph Banks Rhine.* American Psychologist, 1981.

Mcginn Bernard. The Essential Writings of Christian Mysticism. by Paperback, Dec. 12, 2006.

McNamara W. *Christian Mysticism: The Art of the Inner Way.* Amity House, 1988. Print.

Merton Thomas. *No man is an island.* Hardcourt Publishing, 2002.

"Mother Teresa," Biography, updated February 24, 2020. https://www.biography.com/religious-figure/mother-teresa-https://www.artisticdailyprayers.org/teresa-of-calcutta.html 2022

Myers F.W.H. *Human Personality and its Survival of Bodily Death.* Dover Publications, Mineola, NY: 2004. Print.

Myss Caroline. *Entering the Castle: An Inner Path to God and your Soul.* NY:Free Press, 2007. Print.

Invisible Acts of Power: Channeling Grace in Your Everyday Life. Atria Paperbacks, 2006.Micheli at Lourdes. https://www.ncbi.nlm.nih.gov/pmc/articles/PMC6027009

Murray P. *Shakespeare's Imagined Persons: The Psychology of Role Playing and Acting.* Barnes and Noble US, 1996.

Neilan B. The Miraculous Cure of a Sarcoma of the Pelvis: Cure of Vittorio Scientific contributions, Article · Aug 2013 · The Linacre quarterly

Nicoll Maurice, Jay Kinney. *The Inner West: An Introduction to the Hidden Wisdom of the West.* New York, NY. Penguin Books, 2004.

Ouspensky P.D. *A New Model of the Universe.* Dover Publications. Print.

Palmer G.E.H., Sherrard Philip, and Ware Kallistos. *Philokalia: The Eastern Christian Spiritual Texts.* SkyLight Illuminations, 2006. Print.

Peskowitz D . *Neuroscience and God.* https://boingboing. net/2007/10/08/neuroscience-and-god.html

Plato. Great Dialogues 1984. *The Republic of Plato.* 360 BC. B. Jowett translations. Penguin Classics, 2021.

Pope Jean Paul ll. *Encyclical Letter: Faith and Reason, 1998.* Print.

The Power of Now: A Guide to Spiritual Enlightenment. Vancouver BC: Namaste Publishing, 2004. Print https://www.pinterest.com/pin/384283780682138021

Power of prayer. YouTube November 16th, 2013.

Pratt David. *Rupert Sheldrake: A Theosophical Approach.* Theosophical University Press, 1992. Print.

Pruitt S. *Mind Readers.* https://history.com/espionage. 2018 ,2018
https://history.com. 2020
https://quotefancy.com/quote/923788. 2020

Rajneesh Bhagwan, Shree. *Meditation: The Art of Ecstacy.* Harper and Row, 1978. Print.

Reeve, C.D.C. *De Anima.* Hackett Publishing Co., 2017.

Rhine, Joseph Banks. Extra- Sensory Perception, Clarke University Press,1926.

Roth, Ron, The Healing Path of Prayer, Hay House, 1999.

Rucker, Rudy. *Infinity and the Mind: The Science and Philosophy of the Infinite.* Birkhauser, 1982. Print

Salovey, P., J.D. Mayer. *Emotional Intelligence.* Journal, Volume 9, Issue 3

Schweitzer, Albert, *Kulturphilosophie: Civilizationand Ethics* Vol. 2, Generic,1923. https://quotepark.com/quotes/1936132)

Scmidt, M. *7 Modern Miracles that Science Can Not Explain.* https://www.beliefnet.com/inspiration/7-modern-miracles-that-science-cant-explain.aspx

Spirituality, Contemplation, and Transformation. Lantern Book, 2008.

Sloan, J - *https://www.mic.com/articles/98310,* 2014.

Synchronicity: An Acausal Connecting Principle. Princeton University Press, 2010.

Takeuchi Cullen, Lisa. *How to Get Smarter: One Breath at a Time.* Time, 2006.

Tan, Chade-Meng. *Search Inside Yourself:* The Unexpected Path to Achieving Success, Happiness (and World Peace), New York, NY: Harper Collins, 2014. Print.

Teresa, Mother. United Nations Speech. (https://www.pierced-hearts.org/purity_heart_morality/mother_teresa_address_united_nations.htm). 2022

Theosis: Achieving Your Potential in Christ. Minneapolis: Light and Life Publishing, 1993. Print.

Tolle, Eckhart, *A New Earth: Awakening to Your Life's Purpose.* New York, NY: Penguin Books, 2005. Print.

The Power of now. https://www.shortform.com/summary/the-power-of-now-summary-eckhart-tolle, 2022.

Trine Ralph Waldo. *The Higher Powers of Mind and Spirit.* New York, NY: Dodge Publishing, 2019.

University of California. Science Daily, 2009.
https://www.sciencedaily.com/
releases/2009/05/090512134655.htm Website link

Weaver, W. *Lady Luck: The Theory of Probability.* Dover
Publicatios, 1982.

Wikipedia. 2019. "https://en.wikipedia.org/wiki/Eastern_
Orthodox_Church" Website link.

Wikipedia. 2019. "https://en.wikipedia.org/wiki/Catholic_
Church" Website link.

Wikipedia.2021. "https://en.wikipedia.org/wiki/Protestantism"
Website link.

Wikipedia.2020. *"https://static.hlt.bme.hu/semantics/
external/pages/Monadol%C3%B3gia/en.wikipedia.org/wiki/
Synchronicity.html"* Website link.

Zibarras Anna. *Beyond the Apparent and Above the Present: A
Mastery of Life.* Bloomington, IN: WestBow Press, 2011. Print

Zukav Gary. *The Seat of the Soul.* New York, NY: Simon and
Schuster Paperbacks, 25th Anniversary Edition. nd. Print.